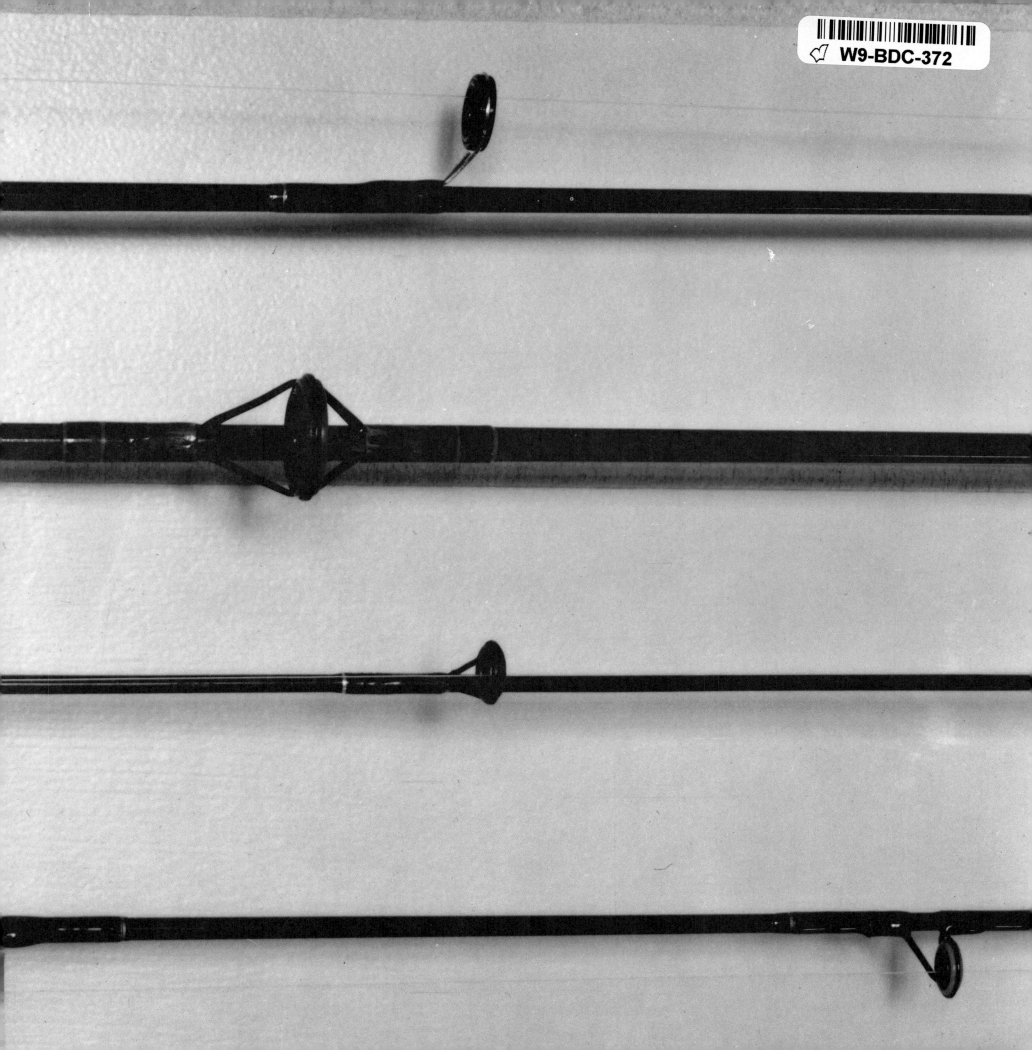

An Angler's Album

FISHING IN PHOTOGRAPHY AND LITERATURE

Charles H. Traub

Introduction by Charles Kuralt

RIZZOLI
NEW YORK

First published in the United States of America in 1990
by Rizzoli International Publications, Inc.
300 Park Avenue South, New York, NY 10010

Library of Congress Cataloging-in-Publication Data

Traub, Charles, 1945–
    An angler's album : fishing in photography and literature /
  Charles H. Traub : introduction by Charles Kuralt.
      p.   cm.
    ISBN 0-8478-1256-1
    1. Fishing—Literary collections.   2. Fishing—Pictorial works.
  I. Title.
  PN6071.F47T7   1990
  779′.979912—dc20   908599
                                                 CIP

Endpapers: Gelatin silver print: John Lawrence, *Fishing Poles,* 1986
pp. 2–3: Albumen print: William Henry Jackson, *Lake De Amalia, Wind River Mountains, Fisherman and Cameraman,* 1880s

Designed by Charles Davey

Type composed by David E. Seham Associates Inc., Metuchen, NJ
Printed and bound by la cromolito, Milan, Italy

CONTENTS

ACKNOWLEDGMENTS

*For Mary with love
and for the fish that got away*

The following people are due some of the catch for their efforts in the research for this album. Without these tireless and generous anglers, many fish would have remained uncaught. Tight lines to: Linda Fritzinger, John Lucas, Nick Lyons, Jorge Nieves, Manuel Schmettau, Stephanie Salomon, Charles Davey, Beth Kugler, Kathy Shorr, Paul Schullery, Adam Sweeting, Waldo Tjada, Aaron Traub, Philip Underdown, Sasha Waters, Arnold Wechsler, and Susan Wechsler.

PREFACE

An Angler's Album is a synthesis of three arts: angling, photography, and writing—each a magical endeavor when performed with skill. While it is not my intent to delve into a profound critique of the nature of any of these skills, I have found each of these arts enriching, not only in my own pursuit of them but also in my sheer delight in studying their forms. As a consequence, I have tried in this volume to collect my interests in the hopes that others will discover with me a new and rich metaphor within the humble sport of angling.

What hold does this simple sport have on the human imagination? Perhaps it is that it brings us into some immediate, albeit temporal, contact with elements of a dark and unexplained realm. A symbolic line hooks into a magical moment of chance; therein lie the secrets of our own fleeting identities and our vulnerability to failure, frustration, and chance. And too, fishing is an act of subtlety that beguiles us even when the conditions are perfect and the equipment sophisticated. We walk away defeated in the pursuit, but pleased at having pursued.

That something as stupid as fish can command so much attention, so much skill, and so much regalia to catch in so many taxing ways defies what is rational—only the poet or comic can comment on it. No human activity is more ripe with humor than angling, and this may be one of its great allures. It humbles the most powerful, distracts the most studious, and agitates the most sedate. The waterside is a stage for an ironic, comic human drama. As shown by a number of this book's images of pridefully displayed catches, the angler's vanity is somehow humorously mocked by the vanquished prey.

Making a good image, whether visual or literary, is like good fishing. Much like the able angler, the creative artist attempts to capture some simple essence of life in searching for an elusive quarry. The meaning of the creative pursuit is the act of attention given by the lone pursuer to the need to catch the quixotic or the fleeting. Nevertheless, there is an end goal, a caught fish or a finished print. The writer by nature is even more solitary in practice than either the angler or the photographer: When he puts words together, he draws on nothing other than illusions stored in his mind. For him, a netted catch rests with a finished paragraph or a perfectly flowing sentence. The writer and the photographer are both engaged in contriving—angling—to make an image probable through artifice.

The photographs in *An Angler's Album* span a one-hundred-fifty-year history of the medium. The images represent some of photography's most remarkable developments and come from many different types of practitioners who have pursued the art over the years. I have included pictures ranging from journalistic records of presidential casts to Aaron Siskind's expressionistic image, *Fish In Hand*, of 1938, and the comic manipulations of mass-produced commercial postcards. Some of the photographers, like Lefty Kreh, are specialists in the field of fishing photography; others, famous photographers like Henri Cartier-Bresson, encountered the sport only as a curiosity. And then there are artists like Shelly Rusten, Philip Perkis, and myself, who photograph the subject because we also love to fish.

My sources range from public museums and archives to private collections, stock houses, and even the corner junk store. The kinds of images I have selected are as multiform as those who make them. Seen here are a range of photographic examples of the technological changes of the medium's development from the 1840s to the present—early daguerreotypes, albumen prints, and the first form of color print, the autochrome. In Harold Edgerton's *Man Flycasting*, of 1952, we see the first use of stroboscopic light. In other images we find hand manipulation and highly personalized arrangements of subject. Photography and fishing both are eclectic activities for people with a penchant for gadgets and inventions.

The earliest photographs I have shown are primarily those of serious cameramen who pursued the medium as a means of faithfully recording the events and artifacts of the natural world. Pictures such as *Still Life with Fish* by Horatio Ross or *Lake De Amalia, Wind River Mountains, Fisherman and Cameraman* by William Henry Jackson represent key works in the early development of photography. Along with the Englishman Roger Fenton and the Italian Gioacchino Altobelli, these artists are noted in the history of photography for their unique aesthetic quest of then unrecorded sights.

These early photographers were explorer-adventurers who sought to discover, record, and inform their audience of the wonders of the inaccessible. Like the angler, the photographer tries to capture a kind of transcendental experience, though with light and film instead of hook and line. The viewer's delight with these photographs comes not only from nostalgia for lost innocence, but also out of an admiration for the simplicity of idea and elegance of vision contained in each plate. The best of these photographs take us into our own realm of angling fantasy. It is important to note that even into the early twentieth century the photography medium still had a magical aura about it; each frame was a precious commodity. This fact often accounts for the clarity we find in images such as the photogravure by James Leon Williams of 1892, and the more topical ice fishing "snap" by Kenneth Wright of around 1935. No exposure was wasted indiscriminately, since the photographic equipment used at this time was cumbersome and demanded skill.

The development of photography and its maturation roughly parallels what has been called the Golden Age of Fishing, the mid-nineteenth to the early twentieth century. During this period, the fisherman's bounty was abundant. Rivers and lakes were pristine and unspoiled, and "ecology" was an unheard-of word. New types of tackle, such as the Kentucky Reel or the Henshall Bass Rod, became available to the masses through retail catalogs like Sears and Roebuck, and specialty shops like L. L. Bean. During this period of increased industrialization came more recreational time, the establishment of parklands, and easy transportation for the city dweller to the wilds. Sport fishing grew enormously and changed from an elite preoccupation of the gentry to one of mechanical advantage for the common man and woman. Similarly, the inventions of the dry plate in 1871 and George Eastman's first Kodak camera in 1888 revolutionized photography by making it possible for anyone to record and preserve any incidence of place or pleasure. Thus, included in *An Angler's Album* are a great many anonymous or amateur photographs.

After the turn of the century, a number of photographic preoccupations developed discrete disciplines in the areas of commercial illustration, photojournalism, and fine art. I have drawn on all these applications of the medium for this book's modern images. It is important for the viewer to embrace the diversity of images as each has an exceptional quality to be considered uniquely as do each species of fish, whether caught in salt water, a pond, or a stream. Frequently for the fisherman, the circumstances in which the prey is caught is of more delight than the size of the fish. (All fishermen lie anyway!) Similarly, the context in which the photograph is viewed gives new meaning to the image. The new context is often very different from the reason for or circumstance in which the original was made, giving rise to a new truth.

It is not accidental that the literature of fishing is as ancient as our first hieroglyphics. Some kind of fishing scenario has been documented even in the caves of Paleolithic times. The catch symbolizes as poetic an idea as old as any the imagination can create. We find in the history of literature active discourse on the sport of fishing dating back to the Macedonians of A.D. 200, as exemplified in the writings of Claudius Aelian. In 1653, Izaak Walton, whose name is synonymous with our subject, laid the foundations for the English-language tradition of rendering piscatorial pursuits as metaphorical ideas. Since Walton's time, a prodigous literature of fishing has accumulated, so much so that it is said that no other sport has been so well chronicled.

Today, major libraries abound with special collections of angling literature. Rare-book collectors scour the antiquarian trade for ancient texts, special editions, and unique manuscripts. The earliest eighteenth-century Sotheby's auctions listed special angling literature collections in their catalogs. This pursuit is not as rarefied as it may seem. The number of great writers in all languages who have touched on the fishing theme is almost boundless. The scribe provides a natural relief for the longing of the multitudes who are kept from fishing by other toils or unseasonable weather.

My choices from literature for this book were made not only to represent the variety and uniqueness of these scenarios but also to illuminate a specific motif of the experience. The metaphors of the typical fish story can include the entanglements of flirtation and seduction, life and death struggles, and competition between youth and age, to name but a few.

The attempt was made to fuse the selections with the accompanying photographs to create a new and heightened perception of this fair game. The pairings of the quotations and photographs are not necessarily illustrative of one another but are intended to create an unexpected view of angling and its aspects. Reading and looking complement each other in the appreciation of this work. The visual image alone is too casually absorbed; we believe overly in the adage that a picture is worth a thousand words. Contemplation of the pairings of text and photographs offer a more balanced view of our sport. (Fish can be caught in a net, but the nuances of fly and rod make for a more subtle reward in the presence of a prize fish.)

The kinds of writing employing the piscatorial idea are as varied as the sport itself. There is a kind of professional known as a fishing writer, who has gained a reputation not only for a knowledge of the sport but also for the development of a descriptive style of "how-to" writing, as in the example of Ray Bergman and the excerpt from his famous 1938 book *Trout*. There is the author who uses fishing as a framework for a story with deliberate aspirations to high literary achievement, as in the obvious cases of Ernest Hemingway's "Big Two-Hearted River" and Norman Maclean's "A River Runs Through It." Similarly, there exists the writer less known to the more widely read public whose importance is achieved in the genre of angling writing. Such works deserve more careful study, particularly those of the first half of the twentieth century, like Roland Pertwee's venerable "Fish Are Such Liars!" or Roderick L. Haig-Brown's "A River Never Sleeps." Still another source of rich imagery comes from the angling description that occurs in the context of a writing endeavor directed toward larger ends. D. H. Lawrence's flirtation scene in *The Princess* is such a passage, as is Henry David Thoreau's discussion in *Walden*. Included in my texts are the words of men of letters—presidents, statesmen, and the like who noted their sporting passion in fine descriptive lines. Finally, the reader will encounter the short maxim or quip, part of a public domain of quotable repertoire.

Today, angling is undergoing a popular explosion, and fishing scenes are recorded in every kind of advertisement and pictorial magazine. It might be said that the domain of sport fishing is the last solitary escape from an overly pressurized world. As our natural environment slowly recedes, late-twentieth-century dreamers seek an experience based on the illusion of a simpler time and place. It is no wonder that so many important contemporary photographers and writers are not only themselves practitioners of the sport, but are leaving for us their own albums of illusions.

C.T.

INTRODUCTION

I am not sure I can remember anything else that happened when I was four years old, but I remember this: my father rowing the boat slowly up the river, close to shore where the current was least and where he said the fish were most likely to be feeding; and I holding the rod in the stern ("Hold tight!" my father said. "Keep the tip straight up!"), and watching the dark green line making a wake behind us in the dark blue water, and waiting, breathless, for the thing to happen which my father said would happen ("When the fish yanks," he said, "yank back as hard as you can!"), and hoping not to fail when it happened, as I knew it would because my father had said so. And when it *did* happen, I remember the shock and the confusion, my father dropping the oars into the boat with a clatter and rushing toward me, grabbing the bending rod before the fish could pull it out of my hands. "I'll hold on," he said, "while you crank him in!" But I was not strong enough to hold the reel handle, which spun away backward, banging my fingers. So my father did it all while the boat drifted in a lazy circle. He swept the rod tip back and reeled furiously as it came forward, did this over and over, gaining on the fish. "Oh, it's a big one!" he shouted, "I think it's a big one!" And when finally he reached down to lift the fish over the side, I could see that it *was* a big one, wet and silver-scaled with great black stripes. The fish flopped mightily on the floor of the boat, refusing to give up the struggle. "Hold him down!" my father said. "Your job is to hold him down!" I lay down on the fish on the floor of the boat and held his fins with both my hands. My father laughed and rowed my first fish and me to shore.

Naturally, there is a photograph. It was made with the family Brownie in the backyard after we got home. It is a picture of a four-year-old with a wet shirt straining to hold a striped bass by the tail and at the same time regard his catch manfully. On the back of the picture, in my father's handwriting, it says, "Charles's first fish, Pamlico River, 1938."

How many tens of millions of such snapshots lie in old photo albums and shoe boxes in the attics of the land? I look through my own shoe boxes:

Here I am at seven or eight squinting into the sun and holding up a string of sunfish from a North Carolina farm pond. This next picture is the first one in color: I am twenty-five or so, standing beside a scale on a dock in Alaska, wearing a wool plaid shirt and exhibiting to the camera a broad grin and a Pacific salmon. Here I am at fifty, knee-deep in the Firehold River in Yellowstone Park, preparing to put a fat brown trout back into the water from which he has just come, but not before holding him just above the surface for the 250th of a second it takes to prove that I caught a fish on that difficult stream.

These are artless images of the sort that are delivered over the drugstore counter in yellow envelopes of processed film. They are just snapshots, hardly worth mentioning in the context of the great angling photographs lovingly collected here by Charles Traub. The pages that follow these words, evocative of summer days and lazy rivers and record catches of times gone by, will speak to everyone who loves good fishing, writing, and photography. My pictures speak only to me. When I look at them, I am spread-eagled on the bottom of that boat again, holding my fish down with grim four-year-old determination; concentrating on a red and white bobber again and waiting for a perch to take a worm; trolling a line in the Inland Passage off Ketchikan; casting a grasshopper imitation to the place where I saw a circle in the dark water of a mountain meadow steam. Photography was not invented for the purpose of bringing back fond memories to fishermen, but it might as well have been.

As I spread the pictures out on the table, I see that they are a record of one fisherman's evolution. The child trolled a bass plug or dangled a worm in the water; these are easy ways of catching fish if any fish are about. The middle-aged man casts a bit of fur and feather, hoping to float this tiny deception so innocently and naturally downstream that a wary trout will mistake it for a meal; this is a damnably hard way to catch fish, and usually it doesn't. Why has the fisherman in these pictures chosen to make fishing so difficult for himself by changing his bait from worms (free) to dry flies (expensive), and his quarry from warm-water fish (sociable and cooperative) to trout (reclusive and reluctant)?

There are other photographs here in the box, and they offer clues to the answer. They are not photographs of fish. Here is a moose—a little far away, but a moose, undeniably—wading a river with two young calves following along behind. I believe it is unusual for a moose to give birth to twins, but this one must have; they are there to see in the picture. Here is a close-up of a clump of showy daisies. Here is a trumpeter swan, only slightly blurred, in flight above a river. It is the Henry's Fork in Idaho; the photograph brings back the day, and the sound of the swan's bugle call. Here are dark hills framing a western sunset. It seems from the pictures that this fisherman now approaches the river with more in mind than fishing. What happened to him?

What happened was that somewhere in mid-life, I visited a wise old man who confines his angling to a certain hard-to-reach beaver pond in the Upper Peninsula of Michigan. The inhabitants of the big, silent pool are beautiful small brook trout, to which the old man casts tiny flies attached to gossamer tippets. When we walked together over a hill and I looked down on these waters for the first time, I said, "What a beautiful place!"

He replied, "Trout can live only in beautiful places."

All these years later, I never string up a trout rod without looking around me and remembering that assertion, which was so true as to change my life. Thinking I was going fishing, I have met a brown bear (also going fishing) on a trail in the Kenai Peninsula of Alaska; he looked me over for a minute, shrugged, and walked away downhill to the river, and I hastened along the path, my heart beating fast, to find another place to fish. I have walked through fields of wildflowers in the Snowy Range of Wyoming to reach a crystal mountain stream in a far valley. I have waded the Snake River in the rain and looked up as the sun came out to find a rainbow arching the river; soon afterward, I found a rainbow on my line, netted him, and let him go—two rainbows in one hour! I have shared my lunch at streamside with a friendly chipmunk, so trusting, finally, that he took the last crumbs from my hand. I have fished in the company of placid elk and skittish whitetail deer, come down to the water to drink at evening. I have learned much about the ways of mayflies, caddis flies, ants, and beetles, whose lives are no less interesting for being lived in miniature. I have seen beavers at play in the depths of rivers (they are not always as busy as beavers), and great blue herons at their patient work in the shallows (all fishermen could be taught patience by the fishing style of herons), and magisterial eagles soaring overhead.

Often, I have been exhausted on trout streams, uncomfortable, wet, cold, briar-scarred, sunburned, mosquito-bitten, but never, with a fly rod in my hand, have I been in a place that was less than beautiful. I owe most of my happy memories to trout waters, and only a few of them are memories of fishing. And larger even than my memories is my anticipation of rivers yet unfished. To paraphrase a remark of Thomas Jefferson's about gardening, I am an old man, but yet a young fisherman.

I rummage in a canvas bag, extract my well-loved and dirty old fishing vest, and inspect the contents: plastic boxes full of flies, one box all elk-hair caddises, one all Goofus Bugs and Royal Wulffs and other attractor flies in various versions and sizes, a box of big streamers, one of weighted nymphs, one of delicate small mayfly imitations, one of terrestrials. (On certain days, big rainbows can be suckers for tiny red ants.) Knife, scissors, bug spray, needle-nosed pliers for bending down barbs, a bit of inner tube for straightening out leaders, a can of stuff to make flies float and another can of stuff to make tippets sink, a pencil-light, a magnifying glass, old leaders and licenses—and here it is, my camera, a German make with a good lens that folds into a leather case no bigger than a packet of Twinkies and is always at the ready in the topmost pocket of the vest in case a moose appears in the river with two calves or a trumpeter swan flies by. It focuses to two feet, which makes it perfect for using with one hand to photograph a trout in the other and prevent a memory from slipping away. I would feel uneasy and ill-equipped on the river if the little camera were not bulging there in the top left pocket above the sheepskin patch.

Photography and fishing go together naturally, as Charles Traub declares and then proceeds to prove in this book. Neither the photographer nor the fisherman wants to let the moment escape, and if he is the same person, this impulse to stop time is redoubled within him. It is a stab at immortality. I once saw an Egyptian angling scene of about 2000 B.C. It shows a man fishing with rod and line. I would bet anything that the artist was also the fisherman.

Or perhaps the father of the fisherman. This urge to cast a line upon the waters and to document the occasion runs in families and survives down all the generations. My father taught me to fish. Looking through the old photographs, I find a picture of one of my daughters when she was young. She is peering resolutely into the Atlantic Ocean from a pier, a long surf rod in her hand. I remember that she was determined to catch anything that swam—game fish, catfish, eel or skate—and that she wanted to stay on that pier after I was ready to go home for supper. Here is my other daughter out West with a Teton over her shoulder, exhibiting a small trout and a big smile.

And let me show you one last family snapshot before you go on to the more accomplished words and pictures in this book. This one was made on the bank of an eastern mill pond onto which I had flung a bushy western deer-hair fly and then handed the rod to a little boy. "When the fish yanks," I had said, "yank back as hard as you can!" This he did. He was not able to manage the reel, so I landed the fish for him, but it was his bluegill that emerged from the water. In the photograph, he is holding it up and regarding it with a fine mixture of pride and curiosity. On the back of the picture, I have written, "Adam's first fish."

He is my grandson. He is four.

CHARLES KURALT

FISHING IN PHOTOGRAPHY AND LITERATURE

COUNTREY CONTENTMENTS

A skillful angler ought to be a general scholar, and seen in all the liberal sciences. As a grammarian to know how either to write or discourse of his art in true and fitting terms, either without affectation or rudeness. He should have . . . knowledge in the sun, moon and stars. . . . He should have knowledge in proportions of all sorts, whether circular, square or diametrical. . . . He must also have the perfect art of numbering. . . . He should not be unskillful in music, that whensoever melancholy, heaviness of his thought, or the perturbations of his own fancies stirreth up sadness in him, he may remove the same with some godly hymn or anthem, of which David gives him ample examples.

Gervase Markham, 1613

Hand-tinted daguerreotype, sixth plate: Anonymous, untitled—fisherman with creel, 1840s

SPARE THE ROD

The oft-repeated quotation, "Spare the rod and spoil the child," has been misconstrued for many a long day, and if I had known early in life its real significance it would hardly have made so doleful an impression. There is no doubt to-day in my mind that this "rod" meant a *fishing-rod,* and the timely cherishing of it in youth tends to develop that portion of one's nature to which the former use was entirely innocent.

Thomas Sedgwick Steele, 1883

Daguerreotype: Hill and Adamson, *The Minnow Pool (Children of Charles Finlay, Edinburgh),* ca. 1843–1847

SKETCH-BOOK OF GEOFFREY CRAYON, GENT.

There is certainly something in angling, if we could forget, which anglers are apt to do, the cruelties and tortures inflicted on worms and insects, that tends to produce a gentleness of spirit, and a pure serenity of mind. As the English are methodical even in their recreations, and are the most scientific of sportsmen, it has been reduced among them to perfect rule and system. Indeed, it is an amusement peculiarly adapted to the mild and cultivated scenery of England, where every roughness has been softened away from the landscape. It is delightful to saunter along those limpid streams which wander, like veins of silver, through the bosom of this beautiful country; leading one through a diversity of small home scenery; sometimes winding through ornamented grounds; sometimes brimming along through rich pasturage, where the fresh green is mingled with sweet-smelling flowers; sometimes venturing in sight of villages and hamlets; and then running capriciously away into shady retirements. The sweetness and serenity of nature, and the quiet watchfulness of the sport, gradually bring on pleasant fits of musing; which are now and then agreeably interrupted by the song of a bird; the distant whistle of the peasant; or perhaps the vagary of some fish, leaping out of the still water, and skimming transiently about its glassy surface. "When I would beget content," says Izaak Walton, "and increase confidence in the power and wisdom and providence of Almighty God, I will walk the meadows by some gliding stream, and there contemplate the lilies that take no care, and those very many other little living creatures that are not only created, but fed, (man knows not how) by the goodness of the God of nature, and therefore trust in him."

Washington Irving, 1819

Peel Fishing

A SUMMER ON THE TEST

But, besides the past, it is well to look to the future. We, too, shall grow out of date. Fishers of a hundred years hence will cast an easy smile on ourselves and on our methods which we think so delicate and so final. Our tackle and our dress, our practice and our appearance, will seem to belong to the dark ages. In the *Chronicles* of the Houghton Fishing Club is an old photograph of members of the club taken outside the Grosvenor Arms at Stockbridge less than a century ago. Look at them. Look at their immense top hats, white and black, their clumsy square-tailed coats, their whiskers, their fourteen foot rods, their heavy sea boots. And yet they were great fishers, those old members of the club, and great men too, picked men, the best of their time. Is it possible that we shall ever be like that? Not only shall we be, but we are: we are, to the eye of futurity a century hence. We are just as antique, as obsolete and as far away.

John Waller Hills, 1924

Albumen print from wet collodion negative: Roger Fenton, *The Keeper's Rest, Ribbleside,* 1858

MADE UP STORIES

"There is no use in your walking five miles to fish when you can depend on being just as unsuccessful near home," Mark Twain mockingly told us. If that's the case, I for one wonder why he spent so much time traveling around. Perhaps it is more successful to say that one was unsuccessful in Katmandu. If one catches an image of a storied place, one's got to go. The fact is, it will always be told that it was better somewhere else and the crazed will have to leave.

Carlo Uva, 1988

Albumen print: Felice A. Beato, *Nagasaki, Japan,* 1865

PREFACE TO ANDROCLES AND THE LION

He cannot allow the calling of Peter, James, and John from their boats to pass without a comic miraculous overdraft of fishes, with the net sinking the boats and provoking Peter to exclaim, "Depart from me; for I am a sinful man, O Lord," which should probably be translated, "I want no more of your miracles: natural fishing is good enough for my boats."

George Bernard Shaw, 1912

Albumen print: Gioacchino Altobelli, *Tiberen Ved Castel Sant'Angelo,* ca. 1868

LONE ANGLER'S PRAYER

Grant me the gentle effacement of malicious envy,
The peaceful retrospection of the true angler's spirit,
Fulfilment of modest, fair-fought and appreciative victory,
And the ever-keen delight in a fellow angler's
Good fortune and accomplishment.
                    This be my prayer!
                              J. Auburn Wiborn, 1919

Speckled Trout

Photo by Roleff

NIGHT FISHING FOR BLUES

                    Let's just fish
all night, she says. I hand her her pole, then cast
as far as I can. She pumps, wings a sinker and naked
hooks into flashing slop, then reels. As if by design,

            our lines leap crisp as daguerreotypes; we have

caught each other out in the mindless deep and thrash
our lines in midair too high for any Blue to know.
Like ghosts cruising the brain's black room
we seem to pull at nothing, but feel a way
to sit on the shaky pier like prisoners. Coil
by coil we trace a fester of knots backward,

            unlooping, feeling for holes, giving, taking,

our skins crawling with gnats.

                                        Dave Smith, 1983

Gelatin silver print from gelatin dry plate glass negative: William Henry
Jackson, *Trout Fishing at Wagon Wheel Gap,* 1883

THE FISHING STORY 'LIFE' MISSED

On the evening of the second day I did get on to one decent fighting brown when fate had poor Bob reloading his camera. By the time he'd shed that one and grabbed and focused another—he bristled with them—the bored brown had wound itself around an underwater snag and, as we heard my leader go *ping*, was merrily off and away.

In retrospect, as I write this it sweeps over me that this sort of thing has happened so often, not only then but since, that I'm prepared to swear that a fisherman is only at his relaxed best when he knows that nothing is watching him except the scampering chipmunks and God.

Bob was most understanding and nice about the whole thing, being a fisherman himself, but by the end of the third day the strain began to tell and even I could sense—in fact *that* was a good part of my trouble—that *Life* fully expected Bob to come up with at least one thrilling picture of a trophy trout being caught by that best-selling fly-casting author of *Trout Madness* because, after all, *Life* dealt in *success*.

* * *

Hours later, back around my kitchen table, I had my final inspiration. "I've *got* it!" I said, slapping my leg.

"What's that?" Kelley said. "That we go make a midnight raid on the local fish hatchery?"

"The idea for your real fishing story," I ran on, all aglow with my vision. "Look, fellas, it's simply perfect. Here's this master fisherman you came a million miles to photograph, the wily angler, the old fox, the guy who writes books about his art—who after four days of flailing falls flat on his—"

* * *

"And there's good ol' Moose, who never held a rod in his life, who threshes around like a mired mastodon in one solitary pool, heaving out harpoons and flailing away for hours like a man beating a rug—and who makes the old master look like a bum." I spread my hands. "That's your *real* story, boys. It's beautiful. I love it. And God knows it's fishing."

Moose wagged his head. "We'd be fired," he said.

* * *

We came to do a success story about a best-selling author and expert fly fisherman. That is our mission."

"So-called expert," I amended.

"No matter. Anything that tarnishes that halo of success—or maybe haloes don't tarnish—or dims the glittering image of our star is bad and verboten. The magazine'd never stand for it and we could indeed lose our jobs."

* * *

That was at least a dozen years ago. Since then *Life* has folded its tent, of course, and Bob and Moose have moved on to greener pastures. But as I look back on it and consider my small part in it I can't help wondering whether *Life* wasn't sealing its own death warrant even then by so endlessly spinning its gilded fairy tales of "success," instead of telling it as it was. At least in its heedless death flight after this elusive will-o'-the-wisp I know of one grand fishing story it surely missed.

Robert Traver [John Voelker], 1974

Albumen print: William Henry Jackson, *Lake De Amalia, Wind River Mountains, Fisherman and Cameraman*, 1880s

CLEOPATRA AND ANTONY

On a time Antonius went to angle for fish, and when he could take none, he was as angrie as could be, bicause Cleopatra stoode by. Wherefore he secretly commaunded the fisher men, that when he cast in his line, they should straight dive under the water, and put a fishe on his hooke which they had taken before: and so snatched up his angling rodde, and brought up fish twise or thrise. Cleopatra found it straight, yet she seemed not to see it, but wondred at his excellent fishing: but when she was alone by her selfe among her owne people, she told them howe it was, and bad them the next morning to be on the water to see the fishing. A number of people came to the haven, and got into the fisher boates to see this fishing. Antonius then threw in his line and Cleopatra straight commaunded one of her men to dive under water before Antonius' men, and to put some old salte fish upon his baite, like unto those that are brought out of the contrie of Pont. When he had hong the fish on his hooke, Antonius thinking he had taken a fishe in deede, snatched up his line presently. Then they all fell a laughing. Cleopatra laughing also, said unto him: Leave us (my Lord) Ægyptians (which dwell in the contrie of Pharus and Canobus) your angling rodde: this is not thy profession: thou must hunt after conquering of realmes and contries.

Plutarch (ca. A.D. 46–120)

Albumen print: Seneca Ray Stoddard, *A Bargain,* 1880s

857—A Bargain. Scene on the Richelieu River. Copyright, 1891, by S. R. Stoddard, Glens Falls, N. Y.

THE PHILOSOPHICAL FISHERMAN

The defeated fishermen never lacks a sympathetic audience, for listeners share his quaint belief that all that stood between him and success was the trouts' jealously guarded secret. They have often found themselves in the same boat and are fully aware of the limits to which trout will go in order to fool fishermen. Here again, the possibility of failure because of commonplace reasons is instinctively dismissed. The unique ardor of the trout fisherman is best complimented by blaming failure, not on his own ineptness, but on the devastating cunning of his wily antagonist.

Harold F. Blaisdell, 1969

THE FISHERMAN

Although I can see him still,
The freckled man who goes
To a grey place on a hill
In grey Connemara clothes
At dawn to cast his flies,
It's long since I began
To call up to the eyes
This wise and simple man.
All day I'd looked in the face
What I had hoped 'twould be
To write for my own race
And the reality;
The living men that I hate,
The dead man that I loved,
The craven man in his seat,
The insolent unreproved,
And no knave brought to book
Who has won a drunken cheer,
The witty man and his joke
Aimed at the commonest ear,
The clever man who cries
The catch-cries of the clown,
The beating down of the wise
And great Art beaten down.

Maybe a twelvemonth since
Suddenly I began,
In scorn of this audience,
Imagining a man,
And his sun-freckled face,
And grey Connemara cloth,
Climbing up to a place
Where stone is dark under froth,
And the down-turn of his wrist
When the flies drop in the stream;
A man who does not exist,
A man who is but a dream;
And cried, 'Before I am old
I shall have written him one
Poem maybe as cold
And passionate as the dawn.'

W. B. Yeats, 1919

Photogravure: James Leon Williams, *While Flowing Rivers Yield Such Blameless Sport,* 1892

34

ONCE ON A SUNDAY

"My problem," said the man, as he and the two charter-boatmen put their heads together, "is as difficult as it is simple. I'm a minister o' the gospel—a Presbyterian—though I wouldn't like it to be held against me."

Crunch and Des chuckled.

". . . At any rate, I've got a congregation of fishermen—and golf players, to boot. Being a Scot, I can handle the golf, on week days, though it somewhat drains my congregations on the Sabbath, I hear. As fishing does, to an even greater degree, in the summer. But I like to know something of the pursuits of the men I preach to. So I'm doubly glad to be able to take advantage of this vacation to find out what I can of salt-water fishing. Have I made myself clear?"

Philip Wylie, 1944

Albumen print: E. G. Harris, *Just Landed,* **late 1880s**

FISH ARE SUCH LIARS!

"Very shocking," said Old Trout. "Cannibals are disgusting. They destroy the social amenities of the river. We fish have but little family life and should therefore aim to cultivate a freemasonry of good-fellowship among ourselves. For my part, I am happy to line up with other well-conducted trout and content myself with what happens along my own particular drift."

Roland Pertwee, 1931

Gelatin silver print: Anonymous, *Men and Women Display Fish Caught in Leech Lake at Rear of Train,* ca. 1896

THE FISHERMAN'S CALLING

The Religious Fisher-man

Your Saviour *Calls* you to Avoid the *Nets* (and *Hooks*) which the *Destroyer* Employes for your Confusion. Satan, Commanding a vast Army of Evil *Spirits,* and armed with great Advantages against us, designs the Ruine of our *Fisher-men,* as well as of other men. And tho' there are far more *Devils* than there are *Fisher-men* in the world, yet because they are *United* in their *Devilish Design,* we Speak of them in the Singular Number ; as if he were but *One Destroyer. Fisher-men,* Tis in the methods of the *Fisher-man,* that this *Destroyer Seeks to Devour you!*

Cotton Mather, 1712

Albumen print: Strohmeyer and Wyman, *A Fishing Smack,* 1899

A Fishing Smack. *No. 1*
Copyright 1899 by Strohmeyer & Wyman.

THE OLD MAN AND THE BOY

The old man used to say that the best part of hunting and fishing was the thinking about going and the talking about it after you got back. You just had to have the actual middle as a basis of conversation and to put some meat in the pot. "Everybody," he said, "should be allowed to brag some about what he did good that day and to cover up shameless on what he did wrong."

Robert Ruark, 1953

Albumen print: Anonymous, *Thomas Barrows and George Reed,* late 1880s

FISHERMAN'S LUCK

It is a plain, homely, old-fashioned meditation, reader, but not unprofitable. When I talk to you of fisherman's luck, I do not forget that there are deeper things behind it. I remember that what we call our fortunes, good or ill, are but the wise dealings and distributions of a Wisdom higher, and a Kindness greater, than our own. And I suppose that their meaning is that we should learn, by all the uncertainties of our life, even the smallest, how to be brave and steady and temperate and hopeful, whatever comes, because we believe that behind it all there lies a purpose of good, and over it all there watches a providence of blessing.

In the school of life many branches of knowledge are taught. But the only philosophy that amounts to anything, after all, is just the secret of making friends with our luck.

Henry van Dyke, 1899

Gelatin silver print from gelatin dry plate glass negative: Charles R. Pratsch, *Two Fishermen,* ca. 1900

Fish or cut bait.

American slang

Gelatin silver print from gelatin dry plate glass negative: Anonymous, *Postmaster & 'Bronco Bill'—Catch of 1 Hour off Dock,* 1901

A ROMAN BROOK

The brook has forgotten me, but I have not forgotten the brook. Many faces have been mirrored since in the flowing water, many feet have waded in the sandy shallow. I wonder if anyone else can see it in a picture before the eyes as I can, bright and vivid as trees suddenly shown at night by a great flash of lightning. All the leaves and branches and the birds at roost are visible during the flash. It is barely a second; it seems much longer. Memory, like the lightning, reveals the pictures in the mind. Every curve, every shore and shallow, is as familiar now as when I followed the winding stream so often.

Richard Jefferies (1848–1887)

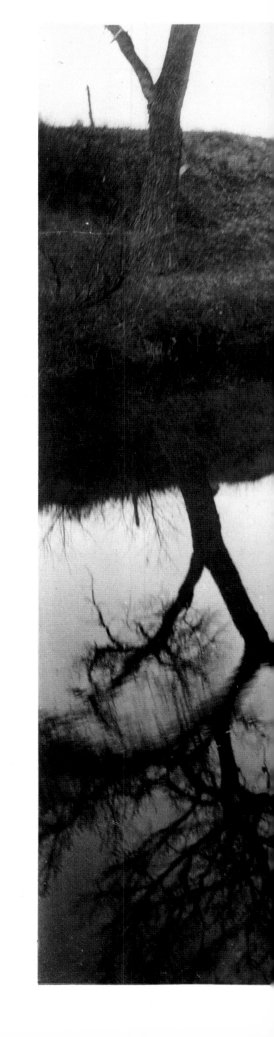

Gelatin silver print: Francis Marion Steele, *Which Will Catch One First?*, 1905

THE WORLD'S GREATEST TROUT STREAM

In closing, I'd like to say to my friend Larry, if he's listening, upon thinking it over, yes, Jane Fonda probably would like the river, although my advice is never to take her or anyone else there ever again. We ought to let something remain.

Russell Chatham, 1988

Gelatin silver print: Asahel Curtis, *Elwark River,* 1907

8396

Nothing is so clean as fish.
Welsh proverb

THE COUNTRY OF THE POINTED FIRS

The brook was giving that live, persistent call to a listener that trout brooks always make; it ran with a free, swift current even here, where it crossed an apparently level piece of land. I saw two unpromising, quick barbel chase each other upstream from bank to bank as we solemnly arranged our hooks and sinkers. I felt that William's glances changed from anxiety to relief when he found that I was used to such gear; perhaps he felt that we must stay together if I could not bait my own hook, but we parted happily, full of a pleasing sense of companionship.

William had pointed me up the brook, but I chose to go down, which was only fair because it was his day, though one likes as well to follow and see where a brook goes as to find one's way to the places it comes from, and its tiny springs and headwaters, and in this case trout were not to be considered. William's only real anxiety was lest I might suffer from mosquitoes. His own complexion was still strangely impaired by its defenses, but I kept forgetting it, and look-

The moment that I began to fish the brook, I had a sense of its emptiness; when my bait first touched the water and went lightly down the quick stream, I knew that there was nothing to lie in waiting to see if we were treading fresh pennyroyal underfoot, so efficient was Mrs. Todd's remedy. I was conscious, after we parted, and I turned to see if he were already fishing, and saw him wave his hand gallantly as he went away, that our friendship had made a great gain. for it. It is the same certainty that comes when one knocks at the door of an empty house, a lack of answering consciousness and of possible response; it is quite different if there is any life within. But it was a lovely brook, and I went a long way through woods and breezy open pastures, and found a forsaken house and overgrown farm, and laid up many pleasures for future joy and remembrance. At the end of the morning I came back to our meeting-place hungry and without any fish. William was already waiting, and we did not mention the matter of trout. We ate our luncheons with good appetites, and William brought our two stone bottles of spruce beer from the deep place in the brook where he had left them to cool. Then we sat awhile longer in peace and quietness on the green banks.

Sarah Orne Jewett, 1896

Gelatin silver prints: Horace W. Nicholls, *Fishing in Scotland,* ca. 1908

A fishing rod is a stick with a hook on one end and a fool on the other.

Proverb

HALIEUTICA

What a marvel shalt thou contemplate in thy heart and what sweet delight, when on a voyage, watching when the wind is fair and the sea is calm, thou shalt see the beautiful herds of Dolphins, the desire of the sea; the young go before in a troop like youths unwed, even as if they were going through the changing circle of a mazy dance; behind and not aloof their children come; the parents great and splendid, a guardian host.

Oppian (ca. A.D. 180)

Gelatin silver print: Carl Evenson or Even Evenson, *Women Fishing From Boat,* ca. 1910

Who hears the fish when they cry?

Henry David Thoreau, 1849

Toned gelatin silver print: Anonymous, untitled, ca. 1915

PLAYING A FISH

A bite, hurrah! the length'ning line extends,
Above the tugging fish the arch'd reed bends:
He struggles hard, and noble sport will yield.
My leige, ere wearied out he quits the field.
See how he swims up, down, and now athwart
The rapid stream—now pausing as in thought;
And now you force him from the azure deep:
He mounts, he bends, and with resilient leap
Bounds into air!

Oppian (ca. A.D. 180)

Gelatin silver print: Anonymous, *Fisherman Netting a Fish at Mouth of the Baptism River*, ca. 1910

THE VILLAGE UNCLE

How like a dream it was, when I bent over a pool of water, one pleasant morning, and saw that the ocean had dashed its spray over me and made me a fisherman! There was the tarpaulin, the baize shirt, the oil cloth trowsers and seven league boots, and there my own features, but so reddened with sun burn and sea breezes, that methought I had another face, and on other shoulders too. The sea gulls and the loons, and I, had now all one trade; we skimmed the crested waves and sought our prey beneath them, the man with as keen enjoyment as the birds.

Nathaniel Hawthorne, 1837

Wt 44 lbs
3 ft 9 in long

caught by
Roy Weidner
and Ed Taro

THE BAITE

Come live with mee, and bee my love,
And wee will some new pleasures prove
Of golden sands, and christall brookes,
With silken lines, and silver hookes.

There will the river whispering runne
Warm'd by thy eyes, more than the Sunne.
And there the'inamor'd fish will stay,
Begging themselves they may betray.

When thou wilt swimme in that live bath,
Each fish, which every channell hath,
Will amorously to thee swimme,
Gladder to catch thee, than thou him.

If thou, to be so seene, beest loath,
By Sunne, or Moone, thou darknest both,
And if my selfe have leave to see,
I need not their light, having thee.

Let others freeze with angling reeds,
And cut their legges, with shells and weeds,
Or treacherously poore fish beset,
With strangling snare, or windowie net:

Let coarse bold hands, from slimy nest
The bedded fish in banks out-wrest,
Or curious traitors, sleavesilke flies
Bewitch poore fishes wandring eyes.

For thee, thou needst no such deceit,
For thou thy selfe art thine owne bait;
That fish, that is not catch'd thereby,
Alas, is wiser farre than I.

John Donne, 1633

Gelatin silver print: Anonymous, untitled, 1913

THE FISH, THE MAN, AND THE SPIRIT

Indulge thy smiling scorn, if smiling still,
*   O man! and loathe, but with a sort of love;*
*   For difference must its use by difference prove,*
And, in sweet clang, the spheres with music fill.
One of the spirits am I, that at his will
*   Live in whate'er has life—fish, eagle, dove—*
*   No hate, no pride, beneath nought, nor above,*
A visitor of the rounds of God's sweet skill.

Man's life is warm, glad, sad, twixt loves and graves,
*   Boundless in hope, honoured with pangs austere,*
Heaven-gazing; and his angel-wings he craves:—
*   The fish is swift, small-needling, vague yet clear,*
A cold sweet, silver life, wrapped in round waves,
*   Quickened with touches of transporting fear.*

Leigh Hunt (1784–1859)

Gelatin silver print: Anonymous, untitled, ca. 1913

Fishermen are not unlike their quarry: they go through stages of evolution. Initially they start out as honest men but they soon adapt.
Attributed to Charles Darwin and/or Ed Zern!

THE KIND WE CATCH HERE.

Greetings from SHERMAN, CONN.

Halftone postcards: J. Herman, 1913

FELLER IN THE CREEK

When spring is not far behind and trout begin to cast an upward eye, and city-pent fishermen make strange passes with their walking sticks, it is my habit to set a bundle of three or four rods and a net handle in some conspicuous position where the eye will fall frequently on it. That precious roll is the emblem of a gentler fascism than the sons of Caesar have represented by their bundle of solid staves. It stands for direct action presently to come, for memories of vanished days, and for enduring friendship with kindred minds, companions along the rivers of home and by streams beyond the once estranging sea.

Ferris Greenslet, 1943

Gelatin silver print: Anonymous, *Two Men with Fishing Equipment and a Camera,* ca. 1915

TILL FISH US DO PART

I am a fishwife—or so it seems after being married over twenty years to a fishin' fool. I married one and raised two and claim to know more about fishermen than a salmon does, which is saying a lot, for fish are smarter than high school girls. I've shared a fisherman's life and therefore know the extremes of unreasonable exultation or blackest despair.

At the altar, I little realized I was pledged to love, honor, and obey three outboard motors, the ways of the river, the whims of the tide, and the wiles of the fish, as well as Bill, the man of my choice.

Beatrice Cook, 1949

Hand-colored lantern slides: Anonymous, untitled, 1915

FAIR CAUGHT

The morning passed. They had lunch. A. B. Totten put on anti-sun-burn cream, then a big hat, then an old shirt, laundered thin, which Crunch provided. She seemed to be—just a darned nice New York business girl.

Along toward four o'clock Crunch felt well enough acquainted to ask, "How come you wanted to fish for marlin?"

"Oh—I belong to a family of anglers. I decided last year to take my two weeks vacation in the winter. Then I'd had a—a windfall. So I decided to try to—oh—to show up my male relations. This is kind of a secret expedition for me."

"I see." Crunch knew he didn't see—exactly.

Not long afterward Des called, "Starboard line!"

It wasn't a blue marlin. But it was a relatively big white marlin. It hit hard, after following with its pointed dorsal standing out of the water like a periscope. A. B. Totten leaped to the center chair. Crunch slammed the rod into the gimbal. The line came tight. She struck—four times—hard—and without any coaching because none was required. In the descending sun, on the calm sea, the marlin—white-bellied, blue-backed—its fins rigid and shivering—hurled it-self high, splashed enormously, jumped again, re-entered the water bill first, hardly rippling it—and tore up the sea by grey-hounding in a semicircle—head and body in the air, tail racing like the screw of a torpedo.

Crunch spoke when it was necessary. "Lower your rod-tip a bit! Good. Reel as fast as you can—there's a curve in the line! Enough—he's taking it and you can't gain on him now. Good. Now reel again—and then lift—!"

Five minutes. Ten. Fifteen. The white marlin sulked—yanking brutally whenever she tried to turn him toward the boat. Then he really jumped—somersaulting, twisting, throwing head and bill against the leader wire in wild jerks while he was in the air, so that his balance was lost and he fell back recklessly—only to emerge again in an instant—spinning and twisting.

Suddenly the line went dead. Far off, the marlin broke into the sunshine—a sea-enamelled beauty, going away fast.

"What happened?" she asked.

Crunch quietly gave the probable explanations. "Maybe the line just broke. Maybe some little fish took a bite at the swivel and cut the line. Maybe it got cut on a submerged log, or a board in some weeds."

"What was it?"

He felt apologetic. "Why—a marlin—a white—a whopper."

For a long time she seemed just to be thinking. Then she said, in a curious tone, "I see—I see all about it. How wonderful!" And she burst into tears.

Philip Wylie, 1948

Gelatin silver prints: Joseph Kirkbridge, *Tarpon Fishing in Estero Bay, Charlotte Harbor, Florida,* ca. 1884–1891

Tarpon Jumping while being played –

Tarpon Jumping, while being played

Tarpon Jumping while being played.

Tarpon Jumping while being played –

TRAVELS WITH CHARLEY
IN SEARCH OF AMERICA

The guardian came back soon after sun-up. He brought a rod and I got out my own and rigged a spinning reel, and had to find my glasses to tie on the bright painted popper. The monofilament line is transparent, said to be invisible to fish, and is completely invisible to me without my glasses.

I said, "You know, I don't have a fishing license."

"What the hell," he said, "we probably won't catch anything anyway."

And he was right, we didn't.

We walked and cast and walked and did everything we knew to interest bass or pike. My friend kept saying, "They're right down there if we can just get the message through." But we never did: If they were down there, they still are. A remarkable amount of my fishing is like that, but I like it just the same. My wants are simple. I have no desire to latch onto a monster symbol of fate and prove my manhood in titanic piscine war. But sometimes I do like a couple of cooperative fish of frying size. At noon I refused an invitation to come to dinner and meet the wife. I was growing increasingly anxious to meet my own wife, so I hurried on.

John Steinbeck, 1962

Gelatin silver print: Anonymous, *Getting Breakfast,* 1920s

MAXIMS AND HINTS FOR AN ANGLER

Lastly—When you have got hold of a good fish, which is not very tractable, if you are married, gentle reader, think of your wife, who, like the fish, is united to you by very tender ties, which can only end with her death, or her going into weeds. If you are single, the loss of the fish, when you thought the prize your own, may remind you of some more serious disappointment.

Richard Penn, Esq., 1829

Gelatin silver print: Anonymous, *Little Boy & Girl with Fish and Creel,* 1915

CHRISTIAN CONCORD

Men fish most for themselves.

Richard Baxter, 1653

Gelatin silver print: Wiswall Bros., untitled, ca. 1917

ARS AMATORIA

Ever let your hook be hanging; where you least believe it, there will
be fish in the stream.

Ovid (43 B.C.–A.D. 18)

Gelatin silver print: Otto M. Jones, *An Idaho Fisherman Trying His Luck with a
Rod and Reel,* ca. 1918–1920

THE BIBLE

A people, these, who catch all on their hook,
who draw them with their net,
in their dragnet gather them,
and so, triumphantly, rejoice.
                    Habakkuk 1:11, 15

TROUT CATCH, MCKENZIE RIVER, EUGENE, OREGON.

SO MUCH WATER SO CLOSE TO HOME

They play poker, bowl, and fish together. They fish together every spring and early summer, the first two or three months of the season, before family vacations, little league baseball, and visiting relatives can intrude. They are decent men, family men, responsible at their jobs. They have sons and daughters who go to school with our son, Dean.

Raymond Carver, 1968

THE FISHERMAN

. . . a fisherman is a lazy bad boy grown up . . . He never helps his mother. He is dirty and disobedient. He plays hookey and won't work. Then when he gets to be a man, all he does is trudge off to Joe's Run or Licking Creek with a long fishing pole over his shoulder.

* * *

You go way off to the brook in the woods or farther to the river. You have a long pole with a line tied to it, and a hook on the end of the line. You stick a worm on the hook and throw it in the water. Then you sit there holding the pole for ever so long. [And] . . . if you're lucky, you catch fish . . .

Zane Grey, 1924

Toned gelatin silver print: Anonymous, *Zane Grey with 450-pound Sailfish, Catalina,* 1924

There are as good fish in the sea as ever came out of it.

English proverb—fourteenth century

Gelatin silver print: Koans Photo, *Tarpon Standing on his Tail,* 1926

© Venice Tarpon Club
Venice, Fla.

Koons
Photo

FEATHER RIVER COUNTRY

While I was stretched out on the bank of the river, resting, a cricket crawled over my hand. It set off a chain reaction in my head that went something like this: cricket; fellow from Sacramento; three big trout. Without any further thinking, I tapped the cricket with a stone. He quit moving. In my vest I had some hooks, and I took one out and tied it to my leader. Then I put the cricket on the hook and let my line drift into the Feather. No trout went for the bait. The hook drifted along, apparently as unappetizing as a leaf or a twig. I waited about thirty minutes before I reeled in the line. I hoped that the cricket had fallen off, but it was still there, waterlogged and coming apart. The sight of it made me feel cruel and unenlightened. I didn't like to admit that I was capable of such purposeless gestures. In the city, it's easy to explain them away. The cabbie was a jerk. The child deserved to be slapped. The boss does it, too. But solitary expanses of country deprive you of your excuses. To be alone in nature is to be responsible in some ultimate sense.

Bill Barich, 1985

Gelatin silver print: Anonymous, *A. A. Cass and the Big Trout,* 1914

THE PRINCESS

Romero, in a black shirt and with loose black trousers pushed into wide black riding-boots, was fishing a little farther down. He had put his hat on a rock behind him; his dark head was bent a little forward, watching the water. He had caught three trout. From time to time he glanced up-stream at the Princess, perched there so daintily. He saw she had caught nothing.

Soon he quietly drew in his line and came up to her. His keen eye watched her line, watched her position. Then, quietly, he suggested certain changes to her, putting his sensitive brown hand before her. And he withdrew a little, and stood in silence, leaning against a tree, watching her. He was helping her across the distance. She knew it, and thrilled. And in a moment she had a bite. In two minutes she landed a good trout. She looked round at him quickly, her eyes sparkling, the colour heightened in her cheeks. And as she met his eyes a smile of greeting went over his dark face, very sudden, with an odd sweetness.

She knew he was helping her. And she felt in his presence a subtle, insidious male *kindliness* she had never known before waiting upon her. Her cheek flushed, and her blue eyes darkened.

After this, she always looked for him, and for that curious dark beam of a man's kindliness which he could give her, as it were, from his chest, from his heart. It was something she had never known before.

D. H. Lawrence, 1922

Gelatin silver print: W. J. Oliver, *Couple Catching a Fish,* 1928

PEVERIL OF THE PEAK

Having reached the spot where he meant to commence his day's sport, Julian let his little steed graze, which, accustomed to the situation, followed him like a dog; and now and then, when tired of picking herbage in the valley through which the stream winded, came near her master's side, and, as if she had been a curious amateur of the sport, gazed on the trouts as Julian brought them struggling to the shore. But Fairy's master showed, on that day, little of the patience of a real angler, and took no heed to old Isaac Walton's recommendation to fish the streams inch by inch. He chose, indeed, with an angler's eye, the most promising casts, where the stream broke sparkling over a stone, affording the wonted shelter to a trout; or where, gliding away from a rippling current to a still eddy, it streamed under the projecting bank, or dashed from the pool of some low cascade. By this judicious selection of spots whereon to employ his art, the sportsman's basket was soon sufficiently heavy to show that his occupation was not a mere pretext; and so soon as this was the case, he walked briskly up the glen, only making a cast from time to time, in case of his being observed from any of the neighbouring heights.

Sir Walter Scott, 1822

Gelatin silver print: Asahel Curtis, untitled, 1929

ICE FISHING, THE MORONIC SPORT

The true force behind ice fishing is that it is better than no fishing at all. In extremis, an addictive fisherman will shoot carp with bow and arrow, set up trotlines for carp and suckers, spear dogfish on Pig Trotter Creek, chum nurse sharks within rifle range. He will surround the crudest equipment with a mystique and will maintain to the uninitiated that there's no sport quite like fishing rainbows with bobber and marshmallows.

Jim Harrison, 1978

Gelatin silver print: Kenneth Wright, *Women Ice Fishing from an Automobile*, ca. 1935

HAMLET, ACT IV

A man may fish with the worm that hath eat of a king, and eat of the fish that hath fed of that worm.

William Shakespeare, 1603

PLAIN FISHING

When we reached the farm the old man went into the barn, and I took the fish into the house. I found the two pretty daughters in the large room, where the eating and some of the cooking was done. I opened my basket, and with great pride showed them the big trout I had caught. They evidently thought it was a large fish, but they looked at each other, and smiled in a way that I did not understand. I had expected from them, at least, as much admiration for my prize and my skill as their father had shown.

"You don't seem to think much of this fine trout that I took such trouble to catch," I remarked.

"You mean," said the elder girl, with a laugh, "that you bought of Barney Sloat."

I looked at her in astonishment.

"Barney was along here to-day," she said, "and he told about your buying your fish of him."

"Bought of him!" I exclaimed indignantly. "A little string of fish at the bottom of the basket I bought of him, but all the others, and this big one, I caught myself."

"Oh, of course," said the pretty daughter, "bought the little ones and caught all the big ones."

"Barney Sloat ought to have kept his mouth shut," said the younger pretty daughter, looking at me with an expression of pity. "He'd got his money, and he hadn't no business to go telling on people. Nobody likes that sort of thing. But this big fish is a real nice one, and you shall have it for your supper."

"Thank you," I said, with dignity, and left the room.

I did not intend to have any further words with these young women on this subject, but I cannot deny that I was annoyed and mortified. This was the result of a charitable action. I think I was never more proud of anything than of catching that trout; and it was a very considerable downfall suddenly to find myself regarded as a mere city man fishing with a silver hook. But, after all, what did it matter? But the more I said this to myself, the more was I impressed with the fact that it mattered a great deal.

Frank R. Stockton, 1946

Gelatin silver print: Aaron Siskind, *Fish In Hand,* ca. 1938

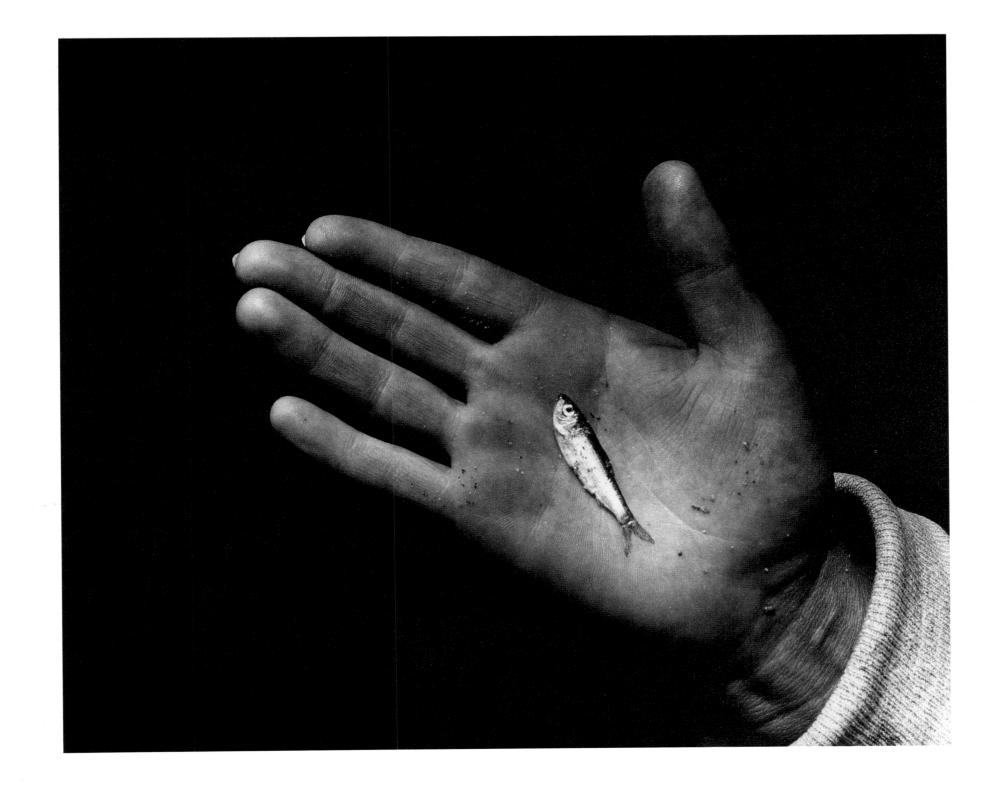

FLY FISHING

Thus, as the angler looks back he thinks less of individual captures and days than of the scenes in which he fished. The luxuriance of water meadows, animated by insect and bird and trout life, tender with the green and gay with the blossoms of early spring: the nobleness and volume of great salmon rivers: the exhilaration of looking at any salmon pool, great or small; the rich brownness of Highland water: the wild openness of the treeless, trackless spaces which he has traversed in an explorer's spirit of adventure to search likely water for sea trout: now on one, now on another of these scenes an angler's mind will dwell, as he thinks of fishing. Special days and successes he will no doubt recall, but always with the remembrance and the mind's vision of the scenes and the world in which he fished. For, indeed, this does seem a separate world, a world of beauty and enjoyment. The time must come to all of us, who live long, when memory is more than prospect.

Viscount Grey of Falloden, 1899

Hand-colored gelatin silver prints: Wallace Nutting, *A Sheltered Brook* and *Spring in the Dell,* both 1939

THE THIRD THING THAT KILLED MY FATHER OFF

Dad signaled, and we got up to cast. I tell you, I was shaky with excitement. I could hardly get the plug loose from the cork handle of my pole. It was while I was trying to get the hooks out that I felt Dummy seize my shoulder with his big fingers. I looked, and in answer Dummy worked his chin in Dad's direction. What he wanted was clear enough, no more than one pole.

Dad took off his hat and then put it back on and then he moved over to where I stood.

"You go on, Jack," he said. "That's all right, son—you do it now."

I looked at Dummy just before I laid out my cast. His face had gone rigid, and there was a thin line of drool on his chin.

"Come back stout on the sucker when he strikes," Dad said. "Sons of bitches got mouths hard as doorknobs."

I flipped off the drag lever and threw back my arm. I sent her out a good forty feet. The water was boiling even before I had time to take up the slack.

"Hit him!" Dad yelled. "Hit the son of a bitch! Hit him good!"

I came back hard, twice. I had him, all right. The rod bowed over and jerked back and forth. Dad kept yelling what to do.

"Let him go, let him go! Let him run! Give him more line! Now wind in! Wind in! No, let him run! Woo-ee! Will you look at that!"

The bass danced around the pond. Every time it came up out of the water, it shook its head so hard you could hear the plug rattle. And then he'd take off again. But by and by I wore him out and had him in up close. He looked enormous, six or seven pounds maybe. He lay on his side, whipped, mouth open, gills working. My knees felt so weak I could hardly stand. But I held the rod up, the line tight.

Dad waded out over his shoes. But when he reached for the fish, Dummy started sputtering, shaking his head, waving his arms.

"Now what the hell's the matter with you, Dummy? The boy's got hold of the biggest bass I ever seen, and he ain't going to throw him back, by God!"

Dummy kept carrying on and gesturing toward the pond.

"I ain't about to let this boy's fish go. You hear me, Dummy? You got another think coming if you think I'm going to do that."

Dummy reached for my line. Meanwhile, the bass had gained some strength back. He turned himself over and started swimming again. I yelled and then I lost my head and slammed down the brake on the reel and started winding. The bass made a last, furious run.

That was that. The line broke. I almost fell over on my back.

"Come on, Jack," Dad said, and I saw him grabbing up his pole. "Come on, goddamn the fool, before I knock the man down."

Raymond Carver, 1968

Gelatin silver print: Marion Post Wolcott, *Fishing Along the Ohio River,* 1940   *108*

FISHING WITH MOM

I learn something every time I go to lake or stream with Mom. It started back when I was six years old, the first time she took me fishing. Mom has a theory that six is about the correct age to start a boy's angling instruction, just as the educators figure that is the right time to start pouring book learning into him. Earlier than that, she thinks, children's minds usually are not capable of concentrating long enough on one thing to make it worth while or even safe to start them. But I was six, and it was our first expedition together. I was in high spirits. My first year of school had ended and the long, delightful summer was ahead of me. I knew if I were old enough to go fishing with Mom, I would soon be old enough to go with my three brothers. A lot depended on this trip; they would get a report from her.

Anderson Cheavers, 1945

Gelatin silver print: Marion Post Wolcott, *Mississippi Delta*, 1939

FISHIN' JIMMY

But one thing troubled Fishin' Jimmy. He wanted to be a "fisher of men." That was what the Great Teacher had promised he would make the fishermen who left their boats to follow him. What strange, literal meaning he attached to the terms, we could not tell. In vain we—especially the boys, whose young hearts had gone out in warm affection to the old man—tried to show him that he was, by his efforts to do good and make others better and happier, fulfilling the Lord's directions. He could not understand it so. "I allers try to think," he said, "that 't was me in that boat when he come along. I make b'l'eve that it was out on Streeter Pond, an' I was settin' in the boat, fixin' my lan'in' net, when I see him on the shore. I think mebbe I'm that James—for that's my given name, ye know, though they allers call me Jimmy—an' then I hear him callin' me 'James, James.' I can hear him jest 's plain sometimes, when the wind 's blowin' in the trees, an' I jest ache to up an' foller him. But says he, 'I 'll make ye a fisher o' men,' an' he aint done it. I'm waitin'; mebbe he 'll larn me some day."

Annie Trumbull Slosson, 1921

Gelatin silver print: Russell Lee, *Fisherman on the Banks of the Columbia River,* 1941

ENGLAND HAVE MY BONES

The fisherman fishes as the urchin eats a cream bun—from lust.

T. H. White, 1936

Gelatin silver print: Anonymous, *Country Boy Fishing,* ca. 1942

SKETCH-BOOK OF GEOFFREY CRAYON, GENT

I recollect also, that, after toiling and watching and creeping about for the greater part of the day, with scarcely a success, in spite of all our admirable apparatus . . .

. . . a lubberly country urchin came down from the hills with a rod made from a branch of a tree; a few yards of twine; and, as heaven shall help me! I believe a crooked pin for a hook, baited with a vile earth worm—and in half an hour caught more fish than we had had nibbles throughout the day!

Washington Irving, 1819

Gelatin silver print: Anonymous, *Craig Turner Returning Home with a String of Bream He Caught in a One-acre Fish Pond,* 1942

GOING AFTER CACCIATO

"There's no fish," Paul Berlin said, but Cacciato went fishing in Lake Country. He tied a paperclip to a length of string, baited it up with bits of ham, then attached a bobber fashioned out of an empty aerosol can labeled SECRET. Cacciato moved down to the lip of the crater. He paused as if searching for proper waters, then flipped out the line. The bobber made a light splashing sound.

"There's no fish," Paul Berlin said. "Hopeless. Not a single fish."

Cacciato held a finger to his lips. Squatting down, he gave the line a tug and watched as the bobber fluttered in the mercury-colored waters. The rain made Lake Country bubble.

"Don't you see?" Paul Berlin said. "It's a joke. Lake Country, it's Doc's way of joking. Get it? Bomb craters filling up with rain, it's just comedy. No lakes, no fish."

But Cacciato only smiled and held his fingers to his lips.

It was getting dark. Partly it was the rain, which gave the feeling of endless twilight, but partly it was the true coming of night. The sky was silver like the water. All day Cacciato had been fishing with the patience of a fisherman, changing baits, plumbing new depths and currents, using his thumb as a guide to keep the line from tangling. He was soaked through with the rain.

"You'll catch cold," Paul Berlin said.

"I'm all right. I'm fine."

"Maybe so, but you won't be fine with a cold. A cold is all you'll catch out here."

Cacciato gazed at the bobber. His fingers were raw. They were short, fat little fingers, with chewed-down nails and deep red lines where the string had cut in. His face was pulpy. It was a face like wax, or like wet paper. Parts of the face, it seemed, could be scraped off and pressed to other parts.

When the bobber had drifted in close to the bank, Cacciato pulled out the paperclip and checked the bait and then cast it back into the water. The rain made pocked little holes that opened and closed like mouths.

"Give it up," Paul Berlin said gently. "It's for your own good."

Cacciato smiled. He moved his shoulders as if working out a knot, then he settled back and watched the bobbing SECRET.

"Give it up."

"I had some nibbles."

"No."

"Little nibbles, but the real thing. You can always tell."

"Impossible."

"Patience," Cacciato said. "That's what my dad told me. Have patience, he says. You can't catch fish without patience."

"You can't catch fish without fish. Did he tell you that?"

Tim O'Brien, 1987

Gelatin silver print: Anonymous, *Fishing Near Lexington, Virginia*, 1940s

SKETCH-BOOK OF GEOFFREY CRAYON, GENT

For my part, I was always a bungler at all kinds of sport that required either patience or adroitness and had not angled above half an hour, before I had completely satisfied the sentiment, and convinced myself of the truth of Izaak Walton's opinion that angling is something like poetry—a man must be born to it. I hooked myself instead of fish; tangled my line in every tree; lost my bait; broke my rod; until I gave up the attempt in despair, and passed the day under the trees, reading old Izaak.

Washington Irving, 1819

Platinum print: Leslie Gill, *Mead Schaeffer, Neversink River,* 1949

If you were to make little fishes talk, they would talk like whales.

Oliver Goldsmith, 1791

*

Lord, suffer me to catch a fish so large that even I in talking of it afterward shall have no need to lie.

Anonymous—Motto for President Hoover's fishing lodge

TROUT

I managed to get a nondescript fly outfit together before the end of the season and started fishing again. The results were far from satisfying. I ruined my chances on every stretch at the very first cast. Because I did not know any better I thought my outfit quite swell but in reality the rod was heavy, cumbersome and dead and the line did not fit it. Besides, the guides were spaced so far apart that the line kept wrapping around the bamboo between them. Of course it was a cheap outfit so one could not expect much but it was certainly discouraging to learn to cast with it. This first experience with fly casting was a veritable nightmare. All I had to guide me was that memory of one cast I had seen made by an accomplished fisherman. Half the time the line was tangled around my body and countless times I had to cut the fly from my clothes or my person. I always frightened the trout at the first cast and then struggled with the outfit for an hour after, fishing water from which the fish had disappeared. On the last day of the season I caught one trout by accident and this saved me from utter rout. With this fish to cheer me I faced the closed season with a peaceful mind filled with dreams of the season to come. For I had caught a trout on a fly and had done it at a time when the other fellows said it couldn't be done. That was glory enough for an unsophisticated fisherman.

Ray Bergman, 1938

Gelatin silver print: Harold Edgerton, *Man Flycasting,* 1952

A WEDDING GIFT

I reached for my reel handle. Then I realized that the thingamajig wasn't on the water. I didn't see it disappear, exactly; I was just looking at it, and then it wasn't there. "That's funny," I thought, and struck instinctively. Well, I was fast—so it seemed—and no snags in there. I gave it the butt three or four times, but the rod only bowed and nothing budged. I tried to figure it out. I thought perhaps a water-logged timber had come diving over the falls and upended right there. Then I noticed the rod take more of a bend and the line began to move through the water. It moved out slowly, very slowly, into the middle of the pool. It was exactly as though I was hooked on to a freight train just getting under way.

"I knew what I had hold of then, and yet I didn't believe it. I couldn't believe it. I kept thinking it was a dream, I remember. Of course, he could have gone away with everything I had any minute if he'd wanted to, but he didn't. He just kept moving slowly, round and round the pool. I gave him what pressure the tackle would stand, but he never noticed a little thing like that; just kept moving around the pool for hours, it seemed to me. I'd forgotten Isabelle; I admit that. I'd forgotten everything on earth. There didn't seem to be anything else on earth, as a matter of fact, except the falls and the pool and Old Faithful and me.

John Taintor Foote, 1923

Gelatin silver print: Burt Glinn, untitled, ca. 1955

TOGETHERNESS

Teach your kid Ickeyology (in English, fish Psychology),
These fish are pretty smart and any kid that studies them will never fall apart.
You'd be surprised what kids can learn from denizens of the deep,
And any lesson learned this way, a kid is apt to keep.
One thing about this fishin, I think it's really grand,
I never saw an ornery kid with a fish pole in his hand. . . .
Somehow it is a basic thing, that a willow pole and a fishin string
Will give a child more wisdom than any other thing.
The best way this can be explained, to every fishin Pappy . . .
Is by sayin, "all our kids are good, but only when they're happy."
This young breed, has a vital need, for a thrill a minit,
Before you put your boat afloat, be sure your kids are in it. . . .
Yes, who can think of a better path to true companionship,
Than to stand on the riffle with your kid and fly fish, hip to hip.
So if to raise some decent kids is your fondest wish,
Just lead em to the water and teach em how to fish.

Ed Stone, 1973

Color transparency: Elliott Erwitt, untitled, 1954

THE ANGLERS OF THE WHARF

Perhaps an apology is due the angling fraternity for speaking of an aristocratic class. The distinction is pureiy an external one of appearance and equipment. Down in their hearts there is no caste among anglers. Go down to the docks of the Hudson and watch. The well-to-do-looking man, the red faced man, the young barkeep, the man-out-of-work, and all the rest fish on in peace and mutual sympathy. How can there be caste among men who trade bait and hooks? And how can there be snobbishness among men who understand? If you doubt the mutual understanding, take your own rod or line or crab trap and join the fishermen. The fresh winds from the ocean fan your face. The ripple of the water comes up from the foot of the pier. The sunshine starts new currents of life in your being. Some way you only half remember the fishing, and like a man charmed by music you sit and feel. Now you know why all the others are here. You know why they speak in low tones. You know why peace and goodwill and, above all, common understanding, make these men fellows; fellows, forgetful of difference in wealth or culture or station, as they sit here charmed by the magic spell of wind and sun and waters.

Leonidas Hubbard, Jr., 1902

Gelatin silver print: Ernst Haas, untitled—New York City pier, ca. 1955

A STRANGE METAMORPHOSIS OF MAN, TRANSFORMED INTO A WILDERNESSE

The pike is the pirate of the lake, that roves and preyes upon the little fishermen of that sea, who is so covetous and cruell, that he gives no

quarter to any; when hee takes his prize hee goes not to the shore to make his market, but greedily devoures it himselfe; yea, is such a cormornnt that he will not stay the dressing of it. He is called the wolfe of the water, but is indeed a monster of nature; for the wolfe spares his kinde, but hee will devoure his own nephewes ere they come to full growth. He is very gallant in apparell, and seemes to affect to go rather in silver than in gold, wherein he spares for no cost; for his habit is all layd with silver plate downe to the foot in scallop wise. Hee is a right man of warre, and is so slender built, and drawes so little water, as hee will land at pleasure, and take his prey where he list; no shallop shall follow where hee will lead. The pikes themselves are the taller ships, the pickerels of a middle sort, and the Jacks, the pinnaces amongst them, which are all armed according to their burden. The master or pilot sits at the prore, yet hath he the rudder so at command, that hee can winde and turne the vessell which way he will in the twinkling of an eye. He sets up but little sayles, because he would not bee discovered who he is, yea, many times no sail at all, but he trusts to the finnes, his oares. The youthfuller sort of pikes, whom through familiarity they call Jacks, are notable laddes indeed, and to their strength and bigness will fish as their fathers will. In a word, a man would easily bee mistaken him in beholding him so handsome and gentle a creature, and never imagin him to be half so ravenous as he is; but *fronti nulla fides.*

Anonymous, 1634

Color transparencies: Elgin Ciampi, untitled, 1960

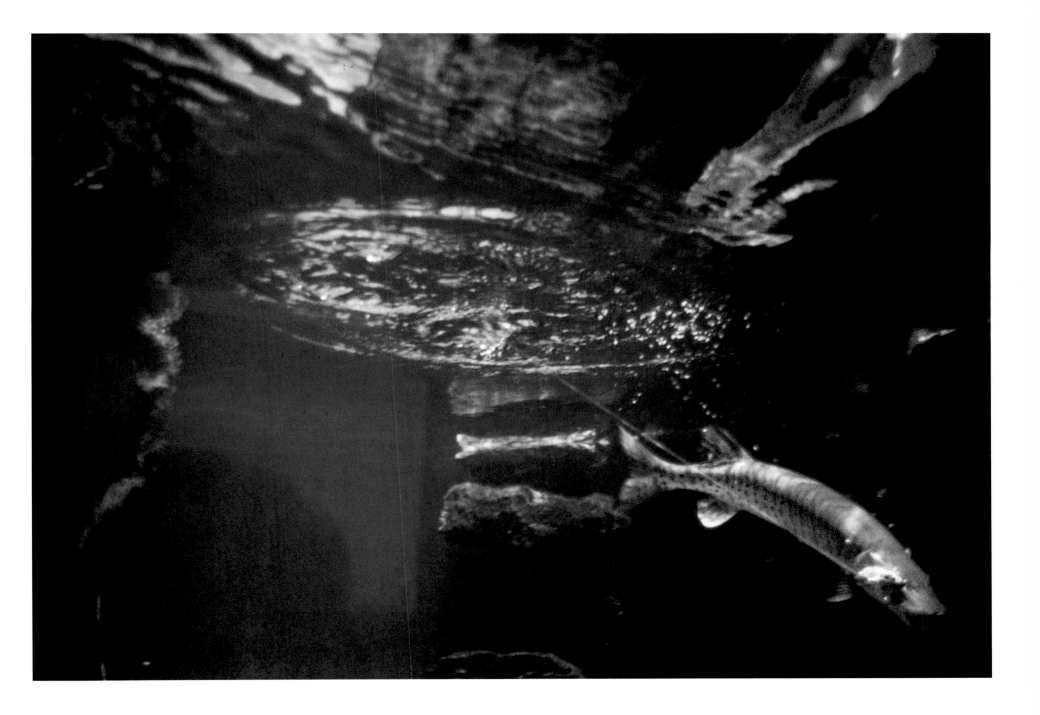

Type C print: Anonymous, untitled—Jimmy Carter at Spruce Creek, Pennsylvania, 1980

Gelatin silver print: James Foskett, untitled—Harry S. Truman landing a six-pound grouper off the Dry Tortugas, Florida, 1946

Type C print: David Valdez, untitled—George Bush, 1987

Gelatin silver print: United Press and Associated Press, untitled—Richard Nixon and Dwight Eisenhower fishing near Fraser, Colorado, 1952

Gelatin silver print: Earl R. Miller, untitled—Franklin Delano Roosevelt at Warm Springs, Georgia, 1930

Generous fishermen cannot fail to look with pity upon the benighted persons who have not better conception than this of the uses and beneficent objects of rational diversion. In these sad and ominous days of mad fortune-chasing, every patriotic, thoughtful citizen whether he fishes or not, should lament that we have not among our countrymen more fishermen. There can be no doubt that the promise of industrial peace, of contented labor and of healthful moderation in the pursuit of wealth, in this democratic country of ours, would be infinitely improved if a large share of the time which has been devoted to the concoction of trust and business combinations, had been spent in fishing.

Grover Cleveland, 1906

TROUT FISHING IN AMERICA

"DON'T DROP AN H-BOMB ON THE OLD FISHING HOLE!"

"ISAAC WALTON WOULD'VE HATED THE BOMB!"

"ROYAL COACHMAN, SI! ICBM, NO!"

Richard Brautigan, 1967

WALDEN

Sometimes, after staying in a village parlor till the family had all retired, I have returned to the woods, and, partly with a view to the next day's dinner, spent the hours of midnight fishing from a boat by moonlight, serenaded by owls and foxes, and hearing, from time to time, the creaking note of some unknown bird close at hand. These experiences were very memorable and valuable to me,—anchored in forty feet of water, and twenty or thirty rods from the shore, surrounded sometimes by thousands of small perch and shiners, dimpling the surface with their tails in the moonlight, and communicating by a long flaxen line with mysterious nocturnal fishes which had their dwelling forty feet below, or sometimes dragging sixty feet of line about the pond as I drifted in the gentle night breeze, now and then feeling a slight vibration along it, indicative of some life prowling about its extremity, of dull uncertain blundering purpose there, and slow to make up its mind. At length you slowly raise, pulling hand over hand, some horned pout squeaking and squirming to the upper air. It was very queer, especially in dark nights, when your thoughts had wandered to vast and cosmogonal themes in other spheres, to feel this faint jerk, which came to interrupt your dreams and link you to Nature again. It seemed as if I might next cast my line upward into the air, as well as downward into this element, which was scarcely more dense. Thus I caught two fishes as it were with one hook.

Henry David Thoreau, 1854

Color transparency: Lefty Kreh, *Trout Fishing—Bow River, Alberta,* 1979

LADY CHATTERLY'S LOVER

The world is supposed to be full of possibilities but they narrow down to pretty few in most personal experience. There's lots of fish in the sea . . . maybe . . . but the vast masses seem to be mackerel or herring and if you're not mackerel or herring, yourself, you are likely to find very few good fish in the sea.

D. H. Lawrence, 1928

Gelatin silver print: UPI Photographer, *Hooked, Hamilton, Bermuda,* 1973

INTRODUCTION TO SILENT SEASONS

You can't say enough about fishing. Though the sport of kings, it's just what the deadbeat ordered. Water is as mysterious as fire: we stare into it for hours, a tendril of drool at the corner of the mouth, lips askew, with little or nothing on our minds. Time is permanently wasted as we fly into the face of reason. You can't say enough about fishing; but that won't stop me.

Angling: An American Ballet. Parts One. Oh, dat fishing! Oh, dat fishing! Me oh my! Good ole fishing. Where's the rod. Ah, here it is, hmmmm . . . Now, for a nibble. Mister Lunker say to hisself, how's about a between-meals snack! Nobody gets cavities underwater! Here's somethin' looks right tasty . . . yaagh! A hook! I fears I on my way to a awards dinner!

Later: What I do with dat rod? Where I leavin' dose lures? Dat wa'nt no fish! Dat was my imagination. Hey, you up dere! Any nibbles? Shit fire! They a rat in my creel!

Wednesday, or The Birth of the Literature of Angling: Mother dog! Dat stream farther than China. Two days and no nibble. I thinks I just stay on the po'ch and reads about fishin'.

This may be a fairly curt synopsis of a complicated psychological process: the urge to stay home and read about fishing in front of a sparkling fire, as opposed to leaky waders and slime all over your hands. Few of us watching Marlin Perkins' assistant, "Jim," I believe, bucking out a twenty-foot giraffe or kicking the legendary black rhino in the shins, want to do it ourselves, whatever the assurances of Mutual of Omaha. Omaha can seem very far away to a sportsman facing the antagonized wild, firsthand.

Thomas McGuane, 1978

Gelatin silver print: Charles H. Traub, *Louisiana,* 1972

OUR BIGGEST FISH

The biggest fish he ever caught was the one that got away.

Eugene Field, 1889

BIG TWO-HEARTED RIVER

As he put on pressure the line tightened into sudden hardness and beyond the logs a huge trout went high out of water. As he jumped, Nick lowered the tip of the rod. But he felt, as he dropped the tip to ease the strain, the moment when the strain was too great; the hardness too tight. Of course, the leader had broken. There was no mistaking the feeling when all spring left the line and it became dry and hard. Then it went slack.

His mouth dry, his heart down, Nick reeled in. He had never seen so big a trout. There was a heaviness, a power not to be held, and then the bulk of him, as he jumped. He looked as broad as a salmon.

Nick's hand was shaky. He reeled in slowly. The thrill had been too much. He felt, vaguely, a little sick, as though it would be better to sit down.

The leader had broken where the hook was tied to it. Nick took it in his hand. He thought of the trout somewhere on the bottom, holding himself steady over the gravel, far down below the light, under the logs, with the hook in his jaw. Nick knew the trout's teeth would cut through the smell of the hook. The hook would imbed itself in his jaw. He'd bet the trout was angry. Anything that size would be angry. That was a trout. He had been solidly hooked. Solid as a rock. He felt like a rock, too, before he started off. By God, he was a big one. By God, he was the biggest one I ever heard of.

Ernest Hemingway, 1925

Gelatin silver print: Philip Perkis, *Warwick, New York,* 1976

ANGLERS' WIVES

"She persuaded her husband to teach her. She was an intelligent woman, and she became so clever at it that she once brought back three trout on a day when neither her husband nor the other men in the hotel could catch one. It was more than her husband could stand. She was explaining how she had nearly landed another when he struck her. They never forgave each other, and it came to a separation in the end."

C. R. Green, 1929

Photogravure: Jim Gordon, *First Catch on the Miramichee,* 1989

THE GOLDEN FISH

Nay, never fear, thou art no more sworn than thou hast found the golden fish of thy vision; dreams are but lies. But if thou wilt search these waters, wide awake, and not asleep, there is some hope in thy slumbers; seek the fish of flesh, lest thou die of famine with all thy dreams of gold!

Theocritus, third century B.C.

Gelatin silver print: Lee Friedlander, *Kyoto,* 1981

GATHERING OF THE CLAN

Our lives are altogether too short; that's certain. As soon as we get fairly started here, away we have to go somewhere else. Worse still, our very limited existence is mostly splotched with worries and responsibilities. The dull drab of business environment is accepted by custom as being its necessary hue. Murders, thuggery, scandals, embezzlements, political chicanery and all other evils of mankind are spread bountifully before us by the daily press like an endless exhibit in a chamber of horrors. Reeking with such atmosphere, it is no wonder that imagination is becoming atrophied. Our milieu carries us farther and farther away from the blithesome realm of fancy. Never more may we hope to have our own "Arabian Nights."

And yet, let one of our present-day anthropomorphists cast off his formal mantle and go a-fishing in the wilderness if you would behold him transformed completely into a real man; a happy child of nature. In the twinkling of an eye the millionaire is mentally estranged from all his wealth and its worries; he is elevated to the peerage of sportsmanship on an equal footing with the chastened spirits of the pedantic schoolmaster, the unassuming accountant, the overtired doctor, the underpaid preacher, the grandiloquent lawyer and all the rest who make up the congenial brotherhood of the mountain stream. Once freed from their irksome shackles, these untrammeled grown-ups are in really, truly fairyland.

Eugene E. Slocum, 1927

Gelatin silver print: Tod Papageorge, untitled—Central Park, ca. 1981

WHAT THE TROUT SAID

Innocence is a wild trout. But we humans, being complicated, have to pursue innocence in complex ways.

Datus C. Proper, 1982

Color transparency: Lefty Kreh, *Trout Taking Nymph,* 1979

Color transparencies: Allan Chasanoff, untitled, 1983

BLUES

FISHERMAN: I brought along some frozen squid for bait. We'll have half an hour of slack tide, before the current starts to flood, and I thought we could while it away with some bottom fishing in the bay, just for a change.

STRANGER: What do we catch?

FISHERMAN: We never know what we'll catch till we've caught it—which puts us in a fix a little like that of the old lady E. M. Forster wrote about, who said, "How can I tell what I think until I hear what I've said?"

STRANGER: Will we catch Picasso fish?

John Hersey, 1987

BASS FISHING ON RIDEAU LAKE

I rapidly overcame my long-cherished belief that to abandon my post of duty in the thick of business affairs for a single day would unhinge the whole machinery of the universe. Indeed, one morning's success with rod and reel converted me from an elderly, serious, plodding worldly worker into a modified savage, content to let men come and go at their own sweet will, while I enjoyed the keen thrill of playing a frisky black bass through the clear waters of that Canadian lake. How many men—and among them men of wealth—there are, who live devoid of a true knowledge of the real joys of existence, and probably shorten their days by reason of an inexorable sense of the supreme necessity of their personal attention to all the details of their affairs. If once the door could be opened and they could be induced to look in upon the feast that nature spreads for the weary and overworn in so many places on this great continent of ours, with its lakes and rivers, its forests and its streams, they would soon begin to partake, life would be sweeter as well as longer, and they would presently discover how marvelously well the world manages to wag along without the personal superintendence of any of us.

J. W. Langley, 1890

Color transparency: Lefty Kreh, *Smallmouth Bass,* 1983

BASS ARE BASS

"A fellow just told me about a pond where we can catch black bass—bass that will outstage any of your salmon." You see I wanted to inveigle Dud. A day's bass fishing with the old veteran promised so much.

Dud stared at me. For a moment his sense of humor was paralyzed. I had blasphemed against his prince of fresh-water fishes.

"By crotch, Mak, yer can't mean that! What's chewin' in your head?" Then, recovering from his shock, he added with a grin, "Mak, I'm 'shamed of yer."

"But," I persisted, "you wouldn't deny a fact, would you? I am offering to prove that pound for pound—"

"Crotch, Mak, a fish ain't a fact. It's a fish. A whole lot of foolishness c'ud be avoided in this world, if folks w'ud keep their facts an' fish separated."

Arthur R. Macdougall, 1946

IN PURSUIT OF THE GREY SOUL

The death of the fish is both the cause for impersonality in the fisherman and of profound regret. Aboard fishing boats there is never any compunction about, say, boating a sand shark and beating it mercilessly to death with clubs. Fish blood in the scuppers is only a substance to be cleaned away, and is not in any sense representative of the living creature from which it came. On the other hand, no one can have seen the dolphin come to air without a feeling of profound sorrow and loss. Here is this quivering splinter of nature turned by sullen and perverse magic from being a combination of incandescent greens and yellows into a mottled and mediocre neutral tone: yes, the thing has been done, and something taken away.

James Dickey, 1978

Color transparency: Charles H. Traub, *Dolphin—Hemingway Deep Sea Tournament, Bimini,* 1984

BALLAD OF THE LONG-LEGGED BAIT

The bows glided down, and the coast
Blackened with birds took a last look
At his thrashing hair and whale-blue eye;
The trodden town rang its cobbles for luck.

Then good-bye to the fishermanned
Boat with its anchor free and fast
As a bird hooking over the sea,
High and dry by the top of the mast,

Whispered the affectionate sand
And the bulwarks of the dazzled quay.
For my sake sail, and never look back,
Said the looking land.

Sails drank the wind, and white as milk
He sped into the drinking dark;
The sun shipwrecked west on a pearl
And the moon swam out of its hulk.

Funnels and masts went by in a whirl.
Good-bye to the man on the sea-legged deck
To the gold gut that sings on his reel
To the bait that stalked out of the sack,

For we saw him throw to the swift flood
A girl alive with his hooks through her lips;
All the fishes were rayed in blood,
Said the dwindling ships.

Whales in the wake like capes and Alps
Quaked the sick sea and snouted deep,
Deep the great bushed bait with raining lips
Slipped the fins of those humpbacked tons

And fled their love in a weaving dip.
Oh, Jericho was falling in their lungs!
She nipped and dived in the nick of love,
Spun on a spout like a long-legged ball

Till every beast blared down in a swerve
Till every turtle crushed from his shell
Till every bone in the rushing grave
Rose and crowed and fell!

Good luck to the hand on the rod,
There is thunder under its thumbs;
Gold gut is a lightning thread,
His fiery reel sings off its flames,

The whirled boat in the burn of his blood
Is crying from nets to knives,
Oh the shearwater birds and their boatsized brood
Oh the bulls of Biscay and their calves

Are making under the green, laid veil
The long-legged beautiful bait their wives.
Break the black news and paint on a sail
Huge weddings in the waves,

Color transparency: Lex Dix, *Bait, Bimini, West Indies,* 1986

Good-bye to chimneys and funnels,
Old wives that spin in the smoke,
He was blind to the eyes of candles
In the praying windows of waves

But heard his bait buck in the wake
And tussle in a shoal of loves.
Now cast down your rod, for the whole
Of the sea is hilly with whales,

She longs among horses and angels,
The rainbow-fish bend in her joys,
Floated the lost cathedral
Chimes of the rocked buoys.

Where the anchor rode like a gull
Miles over the moonstruck boat
A squall of birds bellowed and fell,
A cloud blew the rain from its throat;

He saw the storm smoke out to kill
With fuming bows and ram of ice,
Fire on starlight, rake Jesu's stream;
And nothing shone on the water's face

But the oil and bubble of the moon
Plunging and piercing in his course
The lured fish under the foam
Witnessed with a kiss.

Dylan Thomas, 1941

THE OLD MAN AND THE SEA

He could not talk to the fish anymore because the fish had been ruined too badly.

Ernest Hemingway, 1952

Color transparency: Lex Dix, *Walker Cay, 'Shoot Out',* 1986

FISHING FORTUNES AND MISFORTUNES

Certainly we fishermen are of a strangely sanguine temperament. Like gamblers, however great our failures or misfortunes, we still persist in believing that at any moment exceptional good fortune will be ours. This it is that dominates and urges us on, from pool to pool, from day to day, until we can fish no more.

G. D. Luard, 1943

Gelatin silver print: John Lawrence, *Pond at David's Farm—Bendale, Mississippi,* 1986

THE OLD MAN AND THE SEA

Sometimes someone would speak in a boat. But most of the boats were silent except for the dip of the oars. They spread apart after they were out of the mouth of the harbour and each one headed for the part of the ocean where he hoped to find fish. The old man knew he was going far out and he left the smell of the land behind and rowed out into the clean early morning smell of the ocean. He saw the phosphorescence of the Gulf weed in the water as he rowed over the part of the ocean that the fishermen called the great well because there was a sudden deep of seven hundred fathoms where all sorts of fish congregated because of the swirl the current made against the steep walls of the floor of the ocean. Here there were concentrations of shrimp and bait fish and sometimes schools of squid in the deepest holes and these rose close to the surface at night where all the wandering fish fed on them.

Ernest Hemingway, 1952

Color transparency: Lex Dix, *Deep Sea Fishing, Bahamas,* 1986

THE CARP

I'll confess to a rather rapid readjustment of aesthetic values before I began to appreciate the beauty of the fish which lay at my feet. The New Englander finds the height of piscine beauty in the salmon and the trout. Here was something quite different—something outlandishly picturesque in character, and immediately there came to mind handsome paintings and exquisite carvings by Chinese masters; then came a vision of a procession winding through an ancient city street in far Cathay, and above a multi-colored throng, glorious paper monsters waved in the breeze. A new world of vast horizons opened before me, and on the way home I dreamed of great golden fish bending the bamboo, and I thought—who knows!—perhaps some day one of these exotic beauties may find its way into my landing net.

Leslie D. Thompson, 1955

Gelatin silver print: Madoka, untitled, ca. 1987

BLACK SALMON

Choosing a first-class canoeman from among the throng of *habitants* is akin to picking a winning ticket on the Irish Sweepstakes. I do not mean to imply that the native Frenchman is not a good canoeist. Far from it. He is among the world's best, but the niceties of using a light fly rod are beyond his comprehension.

It is probable that more fish are lost at the net than at any other stage of the battle simply because the canoeman failed to keep his angler headed toward his fish. There is nothing more disconcerting to a fisherman than to find himself holding the rod over his shoulder in the manner of a baseball bat, while the guide has laid his paddle across the thwarts and is methodically loading his pipe. It would never occur to him in a hundred years to turn the canoe so that the angler may face the fish. As a matter of fact, he has but little interest in fly-rod fishing as a means of staving off starvation, when the feat could be accomplished in one-tenth the time and effort by using a handline. By the same standard half a canoeload of fish taken overnight in a gill net would be the acme of sport for him. For the long-drawn-out battle in which the temper of a light rod and the stretch of a delicate leader must not be forgotten for a moment, he has absolutely no use. He seems to regard it as an expression of a feebler intellect, as perhaps it is, and he would be happy if he could convert you to his belief.

We found the Indians to be delightfully different.

Burton L. Spiller, 1974

Type C prints: Stuart Klipper, untitled, 1987

A RIVER NEVER SLEEPS

One discovers other things than new pools and new fish lies in old pools. One learns to mark one's casts by such things as the kidney stones and the flat rock in General Money's Pool in the Stamp, one learns to hope for the sight of a pileated woodpecker crossing the river in swooping flight at this place, a flock of mergansers at that place, a dipper against black rocks and rippled water somewhere else, deer coming down to eat the moss on the rocks at the water's edge in hard weather. All these things are precious in repetition and, repeated or no, they build the river for one. They are part of the background of knowing and loving it, as is every fish hooked, every cast fished through, every rock trodden. And men and women come strongly into it. Here, I can remind myself, was where Ann sat that first day we came up the river together, and here it was that she loved the September sun the year before Valerie was born. Here we stopped and Letcher made us an old-fashioned before we went on to the Canyon Pool that day. Here Buckie brought his first fish to the bank, here I gaffed Sandy's first steelhead for him, here Tommy hooked one last winter, there it was that the big fish took Reg's line across the roots of the cedar tree. . . .

I still don't know why I fish or why other men fish, except that we like it and it makes us think and feel. But I do know that if it were not for the strong, quick life of rivers, for their sparkle in the sunshine, for the cold grayness of them under rain and the feel of them about my legs as I set my feet hard down on rocks or sand or gravel, I should fish less often. A river is never quite silent; it can never, of its very nature, be quite still; it is never quite the same from one day to the next. It has its own life and its own beauty, and the creatures it nourishes are alive and beautiful also. Perhaps fishing is, for me, only an excuse to be near rivers. If so, I'm glad I thought of it.

Roderick L. Haig-Brown, 1944

Gelatin silver print: John Smart, *Storm on the Madison River Near Cameron, Montana,* 1987

THE SEA ANGLER

There was a gentle angler who was angling in the sea,
With heart as cool as only heart, untaught of love, can be;
When suddenly the waters rushed, and swelled, and up there sprung
A humid maid of beauty's mould—and thus to him she sung:

'Why dost thou strive so artfully to lure my brood away,
And leave them then to die beneath the sun's all-scorching ray?
Couldst thou but tell how happy are the fish that swim below,
Thou wouldst with me, and taste of joy which earth can never know.

'Does not bright Sol—Diana too—more lovely far appear
When they have dipped in ocean's wave their golden, silvery hair?
And is there no attraction in this heaven-expanse of blue,
Nor in thine image mirrored in this everlasting dew?'

The water rushed, the water swelled, and touched his naked feet,
And fancy whispered to his heart it was a love-pledge sweet:
She sung another siren lay, more 'witching than before,
Half-pulled—half plunging—down he sunk, and ne'er was heard of more.

Goethe, 1779

Color transparency: Lefty Kreh, *Sea Angler,* 1987

FISHING PRESIDENTS AND CANDIDATES

There are a dozen justifications for fishing. Among them is its importance to the political world. No political aspirant can qualify for election unless he demonstrates he is a fisherman, there being twenty-five million persons who pay annually for a license to fish.

Herbert Hoover, ca. 1929

Gelatin silver prints: Anthony Hernandez, from the series *Public Fishing Areas,* 1988

THE SOPHIST

STRANGER : Seeing, then, that all arts are either acquisitive or creative, in which class shall we place the art of the angler?

THEAETETUS : Clearly in the acquisitive class.

* * *

STRANGER : Then now you and I have come to an understanding not only about the name of the angler's art, but about the definition of the thing itself. One half of all art was acquisitive—half of the acquisitive art was conquest or taking by force, half of this way was hunting and half of hunting was hunting animals; half of this was hunting water animals; of this again, the under half was fishing; half of fishing was striking; a part of striking was fishing with a barb, and one half of this again, being the kind which strikes with a hook and draws the fish from below upward, is the art which we have been seeking, and which from the nature of the operation is denoted angling or drawing up (ἀσπαλιευτική, ἀνασπᾶσθαι).

THEAETETUS : The result has been quite satisfactorily brought out.

STRANGER : And now, following this pattern, let us endeavor to find out what a Sophist is.

THEAETETUS : By all means.

STRANGER : The first question about the angler was, whether he was a skilled artist or unskilled?

THEAETETUS : True.

STRANGER : And shall we call our new friend unskilled, or a thorough master of his craft?

THEAETETUS : Certainly not unskilled, for his name, as, indeed, you imply, must surely express his nature.

STRANGER : Then he must be supposed to have some art.

THEAETETUS : What art?

STRANGER : By heaven, they are cousins! It never occurred to us.

THEAETETUS : Who are cousins?

STRANGER : The angler and the Sophist.

THEAETETUS : In what way are they related?

STRANGER : They both appear to me to be hunters.

Plato (ca. 428–347 B.C.)

Color transparency: Richard Franklin, *Brook Trout,* 1988

To capture the fish is not all of the fishing.

Zane Grey, 1919

Gelatin silver print: Jeff Rosenheim, *New Orleans,* ca. 1986

A RIVER RUNS THROUGH IT

On a hot afternoon the mind can also create fish and arrange them according to the way it has just made the river. It will have the fish spend most of their time in the "big blue" at the turn, where they can lie protected by big rocks and take it easy and have food washed to them by big waters. From there, they can move into the fast rapids above when they are really hungry or it is September and cool, but it is hard work living in such fast water all the time. The mind that arranges can also direct the fish into the quiet water in the evening when gnats and small moths come out. Here the fisherman should be told to use his small dry flies and to wax them so they will float. He should also be informed that in quiet evening water everything must be perfect because, with the glare from the sun gone, the fish can see everything, so even a few hairs too many in the tail of the fly can make all the difference. The mind can make all these arrangements, but of course the fish do not always observe them.

Fishermen also think of the river as having been made with them partly in mind, and they talk of it as if it had been. They speak of the three parts as a unity and call it "a hole," and the fast rapids they call "the head of the hole" and the big turn they call "the deep blue" or "pool" and the quiet, shallow water below they call "the tail of the hole," which they think is shallow and quiet so that they can have a place to wade across and "try the other side."

As the heat mirages on the river in front of me danced with and through each other, I could feel patterns from my own life joining with them. It was here, while waiting for my brother, that I started this story, although, of course, at the time I did not know that stories of life are often more like rivers than books. But I knew a story had begun, perhaps long ago near the sound of water. And I sensed that ahead I would meet something that would never erode so there would be a sharp turn, deep circles, a deposit, and quietness.

The fisherman even has a phrase to describe what he does when he studies the patterns of a river. He says he is "reading the water," and perhaps to tell his stories he has to do much the same thing. Then one of his biggest problems is to guess where and at what time of day life lies ready to be taken as a joke. And to guess whether it is going to be a little or a big joke.

For all of us, though, it is much easier to read the waters of tragedy.

Norman Maclean, 1976

Type C print: Shelly Rusten, *The Beaverkill, Catskills, New York,* 1988

A SUMMER ON THE TEST

By now it was past six o'clock, and the spent fly began to come on the water. All over the surface mayflies were to be seen; they were in clouds in the air above, busy egg laying, now dipping down and just touching the top of the stream, then rising in the air and dipping again. They got thicker and thicker and so did bodies of dead mayfly floating down. If your eye followed an individual egg layer, you noticed, if you could pick her out from the swarms of her companions, that her trips through the air got shorter, and her visits to the water more frequent, and that, instead of just brushing the surface in order to lay her eggs, she began to sit for a second or so upon it until the time came when she could rise no more. Then, her work done, her store of six or seven thousand eggs safely laid, the future of her race assured, she settled on the surface and sailed down upright; but soon she would give a shiver, one of her wings would collapse on the water, until finally she died and fell flat, wings extended in the form of a cross.

John Waller Hills, 1924

Gelatin silver print: Shelly Rusten, *Hendrickson Hatch,* 1988

186

THE IDLE COUNTRYMAN

What a lovely summer dream it is when the mayflies dance! For two years these fairy-like creatures have been living a worm-like grub existence in the sand and mud of the stream bed. Millions of other grubs must even now be below the water, waiting for just such another glorious summer day next year. Ice has roofed them in, covered with snow, the bitter winds of winter have blown across the dreary fields, long winter nights have given place to grey days. Two years for this, the mating dance in the June sunshine, this brief hour of glory!

"B.B.," 1945

IN PURSUIT OF THE GREY SOUL

A human being is holding the string,

*   *   *

A string leads into water:
that is the basic situation,
and of a primeval kind.

*   *   *

There is a division between us creatures. That, too, is basic. We have different ways of breathing, those who live on the land and bring the atmosphere of the planet earth into our bodies to maintain the odd and perhaps inexplicable life that, under these conditions, we have been given, and those others who have another kind of breath. These are the dwellers in water, which exist beyond the fragile and absolute film between the earth-life and the water-life.

James Dickey, 1978

Color transparency: Charles H. Traub, *Striper—East River,* 1988

A TREATISE ON FISHING WITH A HOOK

Also you must not be greedy in your catch, so as to take too many fish at one time, which you may do unthinkingly if you act according to these instructions, which will cause you to destroy your own sport and that of other men, as well. And when you have caught a sufficient number of fish, you must covet no more for the time being. Also you must busy yourself in furthering the sport in every way that you can, and to destroy anything that tends to lower its morale. And all those who act according to this rule shall have the blessing of Saint Peter and of God who has redeemed us with his precious blood.

Attributed to Dame Juliana Berners, 1496

Color transparency: Aaron Traub, *Catch,* 1989

FISHERMEN'S WEATHER

There is a school of sportsmen which regards an alleged preference for fishing in dirty weather as the stamp of true sportsmanship. "Alleged" rather than real, because such professions of indifference to climatic discomfort are probably as little sincere as the assurance of those who go on the sea for pleasure that they find no enjoyment in smooth weather. Here and there, no doubt, it might be possible to find a joyless temperament capable of preferring Nature in her uncouth moods, but the normal human being is for her smiles.

F. G. Aflalo, 1906

Gelatin silver print: Fay Godwin, *A. Willis, Cannop Ponds, Forest of Dean,* 1985

THE WORLD'S GREATEST TROUT STREAM

Sheridan Anderson, my dear departed friend for whom I frequently mourn, had this to say in his wonderful comic book, *The Curtis Creek Manifesto.* "Is there really a Curtis Creek? Possibly, my darlings, quite possibly; but I will say no more because that is your final lesson: to go forth and seek your own Curtis Creek—a delightful, unspoiled stretch of water that you will cherish above all others. . . . There are few Curtis Creeks in this life so when you find it, keep its secret well."

Russell Chatham, 1988

Color transparency: Larry Aiuppy, *Fishing A Spring Creek, Lake Brunner Lodge N.2,* 1989

TROUT BUM

It was a hot afternoon in July when I stopped in at the tackle shop to bum a cup of coffee and kill a little time before hitting the river. The air was dry and still, the clouds sparse, high, and unmoving—the kind of day when the big tan caddis flies would come off well in that hour or so that begins with kingfishers and ends with bats.

Harry, the owner of the place, materialized out of the clutter and came over to greet me warmly—not the usual procedure. He had a conniving grin on his face that I recognized immediately. "Hey, it's a good thing you came in," he said, "I've got some rods I know you'll be interested in and they're gonna go fast."

Now Harry is the kind of carnivore you'll run into in the tackle business from time to time. To him customers are a prey species and he'd try to sell an anchor to a drowning man because he just got them in and they're gonna go fast.

John Gierach, 1986

Gelatin şilver print: John Lawrence, *Fishing Poles,* 1986

When a trout rising to a fly gets hooked on a line and finds himself unable to swim about freely, he begins with a fight which results in struggles and splashes and sometimes an escape. Often, of course, the situation is too tough for him.

In the same way the human being struggles with his environment and with the hooks that catch him. Sometimes he masters his difficulties; sometimes they are too much for him. His struggles are all that the world sees and it naturally misunderstands them. It is hard for a free fish to understand what is happening to a hooked one.

Karl A. Menninger

Color transparency: Larry Aiuppy, *Netting a Brown Trout*, 1989

THE BROWN TROUT

If, among the above suggestions, a helpful hint or two may be found that will enable some fishermen to take a few more fish in the course of a season, I shall be more than satisfied. More than this, one cannot hope to do, for fishing is not an exact science. May the red gods be praised for that! If it were, Henry van Dyke's dictum that "there is nothing that attracts human nature more powerfully than the sport of tempting the unknown with a fishing line" would be but an empty dream, and eight or nine million fishermen would not make annual pilgrimages to the shores of our streams, lakes, and seas. It is the uncertainty—the fact that angling is a game of wits—that appeals to this great horde of humanity, and that is so important a factor in making fishing such a splendid tonic for the body, the mind, and the soul.

Ray Schrenkasen, 1894

Type C print: Charles H. Traub, from *New York on the Edge*, 1989

THE WEE LAKE BEYOND

I was half-way round when the fish rose to my end fly. He came silently and suddenly, and I saw him for perhaps only three seconds in all. No angler, not even my father, could have struck him, so quickly he moved. He came up from the bowels of that pool, broke the surface of the water, cut an arc in the air, and dropped back into the inky water, head first so that he made scarcely any splash. I never saw him again, nor any other, that day. And I was so astonished by his size and by the unexpectedness of his appearance that I never knew how big he was. I know I never saw so big a fish in any Donegal lake before or since. But seeing him for those few seconds on that day was in itself reward enough. Of course I fished on. I went round the lake five or six more times. And I prayed that he would rise again, not so much that I would get another try at him, but so that I would see him again, gaze at him again, be certain that he really existed. When darkness fell I had to leave. And I was glad—it sounds so silly—but I was glad that I had moved no other fish in that lake; and I was glad too, for some obscure reason, that my fish had not shown himself to me again because, if he had, I might have known too much about him.

Brian Friel, 1966

Color transparency: Nicholas Devore III, untitled, ca. 1987

FISHING WITH A WORM

If all men are by nature either Platonists or Aristotelians, fly-fisher-men or worm-fishermen, how difficult it is for us to do one another justice! Differing in mind, in aim and method, how shall we say infallibly that this man or that is wrong? To fail with Plato for companion may be better than to succeed with Aristotle. But one thing is perfectly clear: there is no warrant for Compromise but in Success. Use a worm if you will, but you must have fish to show for it, if you would escape the finger of scorn. If you find yourself camping by an unknown brook, and are deputed to catch necessary trout for breakfast, it is wiser to choose the surest bait. The crackle of the fish in the frying-pan will atone for any theoretical defect in your method. But to choose the surest bait, and then to bring back no fish, is unforgivable. Forsake Plato if you must,—but you may do so only at the price of justifying yourself in the terms of Aristotelian arithmetic. The college president who abandoned his college in order to run a cotton mill was free to make his own choice of a calling; but he was never pardoned for bankrupting the mill. If one is bound to be a low man rather than an impractical idealist, he should at least make sure of his vulgar success.

Bliss Perry, 1904

Color transparencies: Kathy Shorr, *Worms,* 1990

GRAY STREETS, BRIGHT RIVERS

"Must you actually *fish* to enjoy rivers?" my friend the Scholar asks.

It is difficult to explain but, yes, the fish make every bit of difference. They anchor and focus my eye, rivet my ear.

And could this not be done by a trained patient lover of nature who did not carry a rod?

Perhaps it could. But fishing is *my* hinge, the "oiled ward" that opens a few of the mysteries for me. It is so for all kinds of fishermen, I suspect, but especially so for fly-fishermen, who live closest to the seamless web of life in rivers. That shadow I am pursuing beneath the amber water is a hieroglyphic: I read its position, watch its relationship to a thousand other shadows, observe its steadiness and purpose. That shadow is a great glyph, connected to the darting swallow overhead; to that dancing cream caddis fly near the patch of alders; to the little cased caddis larva on the streambed; to the shell of the hatched stone fly on the rock; to the contours of the river, the velocity of the flow, the chemical composition and temperature of the water; to certain vegetable life called plankton that I cannot see; to the mill nine miles upstream and the reservoir into which the river flows—and, oh, a thousand other factors, fleeting and solid and telling as that shadow. Fishing makes me a student of all this—and a hunter.

Which couldn't be appreciated unless you fish?

Which means more to me because I do. Fishing makes rivers my corrective lens.

Nick Lyons, 1977

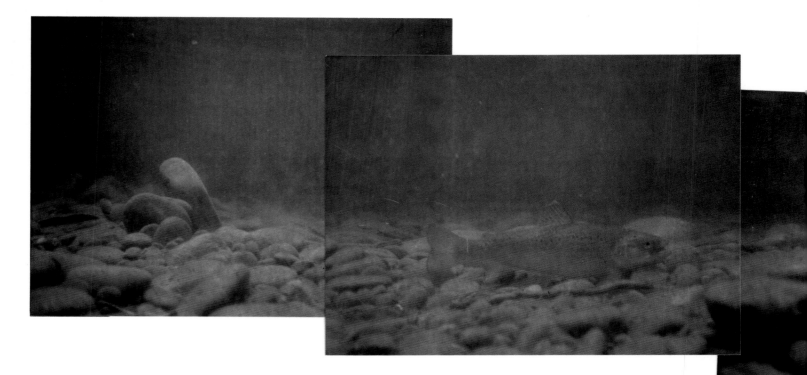

Composite photographs: Joan Stolier, untitled, 1989

THE PHILOSOPHICAL FISHERMAN

The river was full of fish in those days, and I'm sure that skill and the use of specialized tackle would have produced truly spectacular catches, yet the thrills of uncertainty would have disappeared had we been masters of the situation. The satisfaction of taking fish by proven techniques cannot compare with the thrill of catching fish whose capture seems a miracle. This last was my viewpoint when I was very young, and no fishing I've done since has ever been quite as exciting.

It is for this reason that I think it is a mistake to try to cram a technical knowledge of fishing down a youngster's throat. Not only may it sour him on the whole deal, but it will deny him the fun of learning through trial and error. No boy enjoys "doing as he's told," but when left to his own devices there is no limit to the effort he will expend in satisfying his curiosity.

Harold F. Blaisdell, 1969

Type C print: Clark Winter, untitled, 1988

PHOTOGRAPH SOURCE NOTES

Grateful acknowledgment is made to the photographers and collections named in these notes for permission to reproduce copyrighted material on the pages indicated at left.

13 Anonymous. Untitled—fisherman with creel, hand-tinted daguerreotype, sixth plate, 1840s. Courtesy of the International Museum of Photography at George Eastman House.

15 Hill and Adamson. *The Minnow Pool (Children of Charles Finlay, Edinburgh)*, daguerreotype, ca. 1843–47. Courtesy of the National Portrait Gallery, London.

17 Horatio Ross. *Still Life with Fish*, salt print, 1847. Courtesy of Hans P. Kraus, Jr.

19 Roger Fenton. *The Keeper's Rest, Ribbleside*, albumen print from wet collodion negative, 1858. Courtesy of Victoria & Albert Museum.

21 Felice A. Beato. *Nagasaki, Japan*, albumen print, 1865. Courtesy of Dietmar Siegert.

23 Gioacchino Altobelli. *Tiberen Ved Castel Sant'Angelo*, albumen print, ca. 1868. Courtesy of Dietmar Siegert.

25 William Roleff. *Speckled Trout Caught by Bill St. Mary from Stream Along North Shore, Lake Superior*, gelatin silver print, ca. 1920. Courtesy of the Minnesota Historical Society.

27 William Henry Jackson. *Trout Fishing at Wagon Wheel Gap*, gelatin silver print from gelatin dry plate glass negative, 1883. Courtesy of the Colorado Historical Society.

29 William Henry Jackson. *Lake De Amalia, Wind River Mountains, Fisherman and Cameraman*, albumen print, 1880s. Courtesy of the Colorado Historical Society.

31 Seneca Ray Stoddard. *A Bargain*, albumen print, 1880s. Courtesy of Photofind Gallery.

33 Seneca Ray Stoddard. *Lower Saranack, Adirondacks*, albumen print, 1880s. Courtesy of Photofind Gallery.

35 James Leon Williams. *While Flowing Rivers Yield Such Blameless Sport*, photogravure, 1892. Courtesy of Charles H. Traub.

37 E. G. Harris. *Just Landed*, albumen print, late 1880s. Courtesy of the State Historical Society of Wisconsin.

39 Anonymous. *Men and Women Display Fish Caught in Leech Lake at Rear of Train*, gelatin silver print, ca. 1896. Courtesy of the Minnesota Historical Society.

41 Strohmeyer and Wyman. *A Fishing Smack*, albumen print, 1899. Courtesy of the Library of Congress.

43 Anonymous. *Thomas Barrows and George Reed*, albumen print, late 1880s. Courtesy of the Vermont Historical Society.

45 Charles R. Pratsch. *Two Fishermen*, gelatin silver print from gelatin dry plate glass negative, ca. 1900. Courtesy of the Washington State University Library, Historical Photograph Collections.

47 Anonymous. *Postmaster & 'Bronco Bill'—Catch of 1 Hour off Dock*, gelatin silver print from gelatin dry plate glass negative, 1901. Courtesy of the Minnesota Historical Society.

49 Francis Marion Steele. *Which Will Catch One First?*, gelatin silver print, 1905. Courtesy of the Library of Congress.

51 Asahel Curtis. *Elwark River*, gelatin silver print, 1907. Courtesy of Washington State Historical Society.

53 Lumière Studios. Untitled, autochrome, ca. 1905. Courtesy of Hans P. Kraus, Jr.

55 Horace W. Nicholls. *Fishing in Scotland*, gelatin silver prints, ca. 1908. Courtesy of the Royal Photographic Society.

57 E. F. Brenner. *H. J. Smith Fishing*, gelatin silver print, 1909. Courtesy of the University of Louisville Photographic Archives.

59 Carl Evenson or Even Evenson. *Women Fishing From Boat*, gelatin silver print, ca. 1910. Courtesy of the Minnesota Historical Society.

61 Anonymous. Untitled, toned gelatin silver print, ca. 1915. Courtesy of the University of Michigan.

63 Anonymous (North Western Photo Company, St. Paul, MN). *Fisherman Netting a Fish at Mouth of the Baptism River*, gelatin silver print, ca. 1910. Courtesy of the Minnesota Historical Society.

65 Anonymous. Untitled—postcard postmarked Everett, Washington, 1912. Courtesy of the Special Collections Division, University of Washington Libraries.

67 Anonymous. Untitled, gelatin silver print, 1913. Courtesy of the University of Michigan.

69 Anonymous. Untitled, gelatin silver print, ca. 1913. Courtesy of the Burns Archive.

71 J. Herman. Halftone postcards, 1913. Courtesy of Charles H. Traub.

73 Anonymous. *Two Men with Fishing Equipment and a Camera*, gelatin silver print, ca. 1915. Courtesy of the Minnesota Historical Society.

75 Anonymous. Untitled, hand-colored lantern slides, 1915. Courtesy of Charles H. Traub.

77 Joseph Kirkbridge. *Tarpon Fishing in Estero Bay, Charlotte Harbor, Florida*, gelatin silver prints, ca. 1884–91. Courtesy of the Minnesota Historical Society.

79 Anonymous. *Getting Breakfast*, gelatin silver print, 1920s. Courtesy of the State Historical Society of Wisconsin.

81 Anonymous. *Little Boy & Girl with Fish and Creel*, gelatin silver print, 1915. Courtesy of the Oregon Historical Society.

83 Wiswall Bros. Untitled, gelatin silver print, ca. 1917. Courtesy of the Denver Public Library, Western History Department.

85 Otto M. Jones. *An Idaho Fisherman Trying His Luck with a Rod and Reel*, gelatin silver print, ca. 1918–20. Courtesy of the Library of Congress.

87 Anonymous. *Trout Catch on McKenzie River*, gelatin silver print, ca. 1920. Courtesy of the Oregon Historical Society.

89 Anonymous. Untitled, gelatin silver print, 1920s. Courtesy of the Virginia State Library.

91 Anonymous. *Zane Grey with 450-pound Sailfish, Catalina*, toned gelatin silver print, 1924. Courtesy of the Seaver Center for Western History Research, Natural History Museum of Los Angeles County.

93 Koans Photo, Venice Tarpon Club. *Tarpon Standing on his Tail*, gelatin silver print, 1926. Courtesy of the Library of Congress.

95 Anonymous. *A. A. Cass and the Big Trout*, gelatin silver print, 1914. Courtesy of the Oregon Historical Society.

97 W. J. Oliver. *Couple Catching a Fish*, gelatin silver print, 1928. Courtesy of Glenbow Archives, Calgary, Alberta.

99 Asahel Curtis. Untitled, gelatin silver print, 1929. Courtesy of the Washington State Historical Society.

101 Kenneth Wright. *Women Ice Fishing from an Automobile*, gelatin silver print, ca. 1935. Courtesy of the Minnesota Historical Society.

103 Henri Cartier-Bresson. *On the Banks of the Marne*, gelatin silver print, 1938. Courtesy of the artist, and courtesy of Christies.

105 Aaron Siskind. *Fish in Hand*, gelatin silver print, ca. 1938. Courtesy of the artist.

LITERATURE SOURCE NOTES

Grateful acknowledgment is made to the authors and publishers named in these notes for permission to reproduce copyrighted material on the pages indicated at left.

12 Gervase Markham. "Countrey Contentments." In *English Angling Literature*, edited by Kenneth Mansfield. London: Claxton Publishing Co., 1954.

14 Thomas Sedgwick Steele. "Spare the Rod." In *Fishing with the Fly* by Charles F. Orvis and A. Nelson Cheney. New York: Houghton, Mifflin Co., 1883.

16 Washington Irving. *Sketch-Book of Geoffrey Crayon, Gent.* Edited by Haskell Springer. Boston: Twayne Publishers, 1978.

18 John Waller Hills. *A Summer on the Test.* New York: Nick Lyons Books, 1983. Reprint. Piscataway, NJ: Winchester Press, 1987. Used by permission of Lyons & Burford Publishers.

20 Carlo Uva. *Made Up Stories.* New York: Lancaster Press, 1988.

22 George Bernard Shaw. *Preface to Androcles and the Lion* in *The Works of George Bernard Shaw*, no. 14. London: Constable & Co., 1951.

24 J. Auburn Wiborn. "Lone Angler's Prayer." In *Fisherman's Verse*, edited by William Haynes and Joseph Harrison. New York: Duffield and Co., 1919.

26 Dave Smith. "Night Fishing for Blues." In *Grey Soldiers*. Winston-Salem, NC: Stuart Wright, 1983.

28 Robert Traver [John Voelker]. "The Fishing Story 'Life' Missed." In *Trout Magic*. New York: Crown Publishers, 1974.

30 Plutarch. *Cleopatra and Antony.* In *Great Angling Stories*, edited by John M. Dickie. Edinburgh: W. & R. Chambers, 1988.

32 Harold F. Blaisdell. *The Philosophical Fisherman.* New York: Nick Lyons Books, 1969. Used by permission of Lyons & Burford Publishers.

34 W. B. Yeats. "The Fisherman." In *The Collected Poems of W. B. Yeats.* London: Macmillan, 1971.

36 Philip Wylie. "Once on a Sunday." In *Great Fishing Stories*, compiled by Edwin Valentine Mitchell. Garden City, NY: Doubleday & Co., 1946.

38 Roland Pertwee. *Fish Are Such Liars!* London: William Heinemann, 1931. Permission granted by Curtis Brown Ltd., London.

40 Cotton Mather. *The Fisherman's Calling: A Brief Essay to Save the Great Interests of Religion Among Our Fishermen.* Boston: privately published, 1712.

42 Robert Ruark. *The Old Man and the Boy.* New York: Henry Holt and Co., 1957. Reprint. Harrison, PA: Stackpole Books, 1989.

44 Henry van Dyke. *Fisherman's Luck.* New York: Charles Scribner's Sons, 1899.

48 Richard Jefferies. "A Roman Brook." In *Life of the Field*, from *The Fisherman's Bedside Book.* Suffolk, England: Boydell Press, 1985.

50 Russell Chatham. "The World's Greatest Trout Stream" in *Dark Waters.* Livingston, Montana: Clark City Press, 1988.

54 Sarah Orne Jewett. *The Country of the Pointed Firs.* Garden City, NY: Anchor Books, 1956.

56 Proverb noted in *Instructions to a Young Sportsman* by Samuel Johnson. In *The Works of Samuel Johnson.* New Haven: Yale University Press, 1958.

58 Oppian. *Halieutica.* Translated by John Jones. In *The Art of Angling*, vol. 1, edited by Kenneth Mansfield. London: Claxton Publishing Co., 1954.

60 Henry David Thoreau. *A Week on the Concord and Merrimack Rivers.* New York: Crowell, 1961.

62 Oppian. "Playing a Fish." In *Halieutica.* Translated by John Jones. In *The Art of Angling*, vol. 1, edited by Kenneth Mansfield. London: Claxton Publishing Co., 1954.

64 Nathaniel Hawthorne. "The Village Uncle." In *Twice Told Tales.* Columbus, Ohio: Ohio State University Press, 1974.

66 John Donne. "The Baite." In *Complete Poetry and Selected Prose*, edited by John Hayward. London: The Nonesuch Press, 1967.

68 Leigh Hunt. "The Fish, the Man, and the Spirit." In *The Fisherman's Fireside Book*, edited by Clive Gannon. London: William Heinemann, 1961.

70 Attributed to Charles Darwin and/or Ed Zern. In *Made Up Stories* by Carlo Uva. New York: Lancaster Press, 1988.

72 Ferris Greenslet. "Feller in the Creek." In *Atlantic Monthly*, 1943. Reprinted in *Angler's Choice.* New York: Macmillan, 1947.

74 Beatrice Cook. "Till Fish Us Do Part." In *The Confessions of a Fisherman's Wife.* New York: William Morrow & Co., 1949.

76 Philip Wylie. "Fair-Caught." In *Stories of Florida Fishing* by Crunch and Des. New York: Rinehart & Co., 1948.

78 John Steinbeck. *Travels with Charley in Search of America.* New York: Viking Press, 1962.

80 Richard Penn, Esq. *Maxims and Hints for an Angler.* London: John Murray, 1883.

82 Richard Baxter. *Christian Concord.* Boston: Privately published.

84 Ovid. *Ars Amatoria.* Translated by Peter Green. London: Penguin Books, 1988.

86 *The Jerusalem Bible*, Readers Edition. Garden City, NY: Doubleday & Co., 1968.

88 Raymond Carver. "So Much Water So Close to Home." In *Where I'm Calling From.* New York: Random House, Vintage Books, 1989.

90 Zane Grey. "The Fisherman." In *Outdoor America* magazine (July 1924).

94 Bill Barich. "Feather River Country." In *The New Yorker* magazine (August, 26, 1985).

96 D. H. Lawrence. "The Princess." In *The Complete Short Stories*, vol. 1. London: William Heinemann, 1955.

98 Sir Walter Scott. "Peveril of the Peak." In *The Works of Sir Walter Scott.* Boston and New York: Houghton, Mifflin Co., 1913.

100 Jim Harrison. "Ice Fishing, the Moronic Sport." In *Silent Seasons*, edited by Russell Chatham. Livingston, Montana: Clark City Press, 1978.

102 William Shakespeare. *Hamlet.* Cambridge: Cambridge University Press, 1936.

104 Frank R. Stockton. "Plain Fishing." In *Great Fishing Stories*, compiled by Edwin Valentine Mitchell. Garden City, NY: Doubleday & Co., 1946.

106 Viscount Grey of Falloden. *Fly Fishing.* London: Hadden Hall Library, 1930.

108 Raymond Carver. "The Third Thing That Killed My Father Off." In *Where I'm Calling From.* New York: Random House, Vintage Books, 1989.

110 Anderson Cheavers. "Fishing With Mom." In *Anthology of Fishing Adventures*, compiled by Outdoor Life. New York: Grosset & Dunlap, 1945.

112 Annie Trumbull Slosson. *Fishin' Jimmy.* New York: Charles Scribner's Sons, 1921.

114 T[erence] H[anbury] White. *England Have My Bones.* London: Collins, 1936.

116 Washington Irving. *Sketch-Book of Geoffrey Crayon, Gent.* Edited by Haskell Springer. Boston: Twayne Publishers, 1978.

118 Tim O'Brien. *Going After Cacciato.* New York: Dell, 1987. Used by permission of Delacorte Press/Seymour Lawrence, a division of Bantam, Doubleday, Dell Publishing Group, Inc.

120 Washington Irving. *Sketch-Book of Geoffrey Crayon, Gent.* Edited by Haskell Springer. Boston: Twayne Publishers, 1978.

122 Oliver Goldsmith. Quoted in *The Life of Samuel Johnson L.L.D.* by James Boswell. New York: Modern Library, 1931.

124 Ray Bergman. *Trout.* Philadelphia, PA: The Penn Publishing Co., 1938.

126 John Taintor Foote. "A Wedding Gift." In *Fisherman's Bounty: A Treasury of Fascinating Lore & The Finest Stories from the Angling World,* edited by Nick Lyons. New York: Simon & Schuster, Fireside Editions, 1988.

128 Ed Stone. "Togetherness." In *Odious Odes for Fishermen.* Glenco, Wyoming: Privately published.

130 Leonidas Hubbard, Jr. "The Anglers of the Wharf." In *Fishing in North America 1876–1910,* compiled by Frank Oppel. Secaucus, NJ: Castle Books, 1986.

132 Anonymous. "A Strange Metamorphosis of Man, Transformed into a Wildernesse." In *The Magic Wheel.* London: William Heinemann, 1985.

134 Grover Cleveland. *Fishing and Shooting Sketches.* New York: The Outing Publishing Co., 1906.

135 Richard Brautigan. *Trout Fishing in America.* New York: Dell, 1967.

136 Henry David Thoreau. *Walden.* New York: Penguin Books, 1943.

138 D. H. Lawrence. *Lady Chatterly's Lover.* London: Martin Secker, 1932.

140 Thomas McGuane. Introduction to *Three Short Stories* in *Silent Seasons.* Livingston, Montana: Clark City Press, 1978.

142 Eugene Field. "Our Biggest Fish." In *The Writings in Prose and Verse.* New York: Charles Scribner's Sons, 1898.

144 Ernest Hemingway. "Big Two-Hearted River." In *In Our Time.* Garden City, NY: Doubleday & Co., 1946. Reprinted with permission of Charles Scribner's Sons, an imprint of Macmillan Publishing Company.

146 C. R. Green. "Anglers' Wives." In *Great Angling Stories.* Edinburgh: W. & R. Chambers, 1988.

148 Theocritus. "The Golden Fish." Translated by Andrew Lang. Reprinted in *A Treasury of Fishing Stories,* edited by Charles E. Goodspeed. New York: A. S. Barner & Co., 1946.

150 Eugene E. Slocum. "Gathering of the Clan." In *Great Fishing Stories,* compiled by Edwin Valentine Mitchell. Garden City, NY: Doubleday & Co., 1946.

152 Datus C. Proper. *What the Trout Said.* New York: Alfred A. Knopf, 1982.

155 John Hersey. *Blues.* New York: Alfred A. Knopf, 1987.

156 J. W. Langley. "Bass Fishing on Rideau Lake." In *Fishing, North America 1876–1910,* edited by Frank Oppel. Secaucus, NJ: Castle Books, 1986.

158 Arthur R. Macdougall. "Bass are Bass." In *Dud Dean and His Country.* New York: Guard McCain, 1946.

160 James Dickey. *In Pursuit of the Grey Soul.* Privately published, 1978.

162/ Dylan Thomas. "Ballad of the Long-legged Bait." In *The Poems of Dylan*
163 *Thomas,* edited by Daniel Jones. New York: New Directions, 1952.

164 Ernest Hemingway. *The Old Man and the Sea.* New York: Scribner Classic, 1986. Reprinted with permission of Charles Scribner's Sons, an imprint of Macmillan Publishing Company.

166 G. D. Luard. *Fishing Fortunes and Misfortunes.* London: Faber & Faber, 1943.

168 Ernest Hemingway. *The Old Man and the Sea.* New York: Scribner Classic, 1986. Reprinted with permission of Charles Scribner's Sons, an imprint of Macmillan Publishing Company.

170 Leslie D. Thompson. "The Carp." In *Fishing in New England.* Andover, England: Eyre & Spottiswoode, 1955.

172 Burton L. Spiller. *Black Salmon.* Piscataway, NJ: Winchester Press, 1974.

174 Roderick L. Haig-Brown. *A River Never Sleeps.* New York: Nick Lyons Books, 1944.

176 Goethe. "The Sea Angler." In *Poetic Works of J. W. Goethe,* translated by Martin Swales. London: Oxford University Press, 1975.

178 Herbert Hoover. *Fishing for Fun and to Wash Your Soul.* New York: Random House, 1963.

180 Plato. *The Sophist* in *The Collected Dialogues of Plato.* Translated by F. M. Cornford. Princeton, NJ: Princeton University Press, 1961.

182 Zane Grey. In *Great Fishing Stories,* compiled by Edwin Valentine Mitchell. Garden City, NY: Doubleday & Co., 1946.

184 Norman Maclean. *A River Runs Through It.* Chicago and London: University of Chicago Press, 1976.

186 John Waller Hills. *A Summer on the Test.* New York: Nick Lyons Books, 1983. Reprint. Piscataway: NJ: Winchester Press, 1987.

188 B.B. "The Idle Countryman." In *The Fisherman's Bedside Book.* Suffolk, England: Boydell Press, 1945.

190 James Dickey. *In Pursuit of the Grey Soul.* Privately published, 1978.

192 Attributed to Dame Juliana Berners. *A Treatise on Fishing with a Hook.* Rendered into Modern English by William Van Wyck. Croton-on-Hudson, NY: North River Press, 1979.

194 F. G. Aflalo. *Fishermen's Weather.* London: Adam and Charles Black, 1906.

196 Russell Chatham. "The World's Greatest Trout Stream." In *Dark Waters.* Livingston, Montana: Clark City Press, 1988.

198 John Gierach. *Trout Bum.* Boulder, CO: Pruett Publishing Co., 1986.

200 Karl A. Menninger. Quoted in *The Chosen* by Chaim Potok. New York: Simon & Schuster, 1967.

202 Ray Schrenkasen. "The Brown Trout." In *Angling Success,* edited by Mortimer Norton. New York: Macmillan, 1935.

204 Brian Friel. "The Wee Lake Beyond." In *The Gold in the Sea.* Garden City, NY: Doubleday & Co., 1966.

206 Bliss Perry. "Fishing with a Worm." In *Atlantic Monthly* (May 1904). Reprinted in *Angler's Choice.* New York: Macmillan, 1947.

208 Nick Lyons. "Gray Streets, Bright Rivers." In *Bright Rivers: Celebrations of Rivers and Fly-Fishing.* New York: Simon & Schuster, Fireside Editions, 1988.

210 Harold F. Blaisdell. *The Philosophical Fisherman.* Boston: Houghton, Mifflan Co., 1969. Used by permission of Lyons & Burford Publishers.